Night ■ *La nuit* ■ Die Nacht

Photographs of Magnum Photos • *Photographies de Magnum Photos* • **Fotografien von Magnum Photos**

TERRAIL PHOTO

Editor: Jean-Claude Dubost
Desk Editor: Caroline Broué in liaison with Magnum Photos' team
Cover design: Gérard Lo Monaco and Laurence Moinot
Graphic design: Véronique Rossi
Iconographic and artistic coordination at Magnum Photos:
Marie-Christine Biebuyck, Agnès Sire, assisted by Philippe Devernay
English translation: Ann Sautier-Greening
Photoengraving: Litho Service T. Zamboni, Verona

The Art Book Subsidiary of BAYARD PRESSE SA

ISBN 2-87939-155-5
English edition: © 1998
Publication number: 196
Printed in Italy

Direction éditoriale : Jean-Claude Dubost
Suivi éditorial : Caroline Broué en liaison avec l'équipe de Magnum Photos
Conception et réalisation de couverture : Gérard Lo Monaco et Laurence Moinot
Conception et réalisation graphique : Véronique Rossi
Direction iconographique et artistique à Magnum Photos :
Marie-Christine Biebuyck, Agnès Sire, assistées de Philippe Devernay
Traduction anglaise : Ann Sautier-Greening
Traduction allemande : Inge Hanneforth
Photogravure : Litho Service T. Zamboni, Vérone

La filiale Livres d'art de BAYARD PRESSE SA

ISBN 2-87939-153-9
N° d'éditeur : 196
Dépôt légal : mars 1998
Imprimé en Italie

Verlegerische Leitung: Jean-Claude Dubost
Verantwortlich für die Ausgabe: Caroline Broué
in Zusammenarbeit mit dem Magnum Photos Team
Umschlaggestaltung: Gérard Lo Monaco und Laurence Moinot
Buchgestaltung: Véronique Rossi
Bildredaktion und grafische Gestaltung für Magnum Photos:
Marie-Christine Biebuyck, Agnès Sire; Assistent: Philippe Devernay
Deutsche Übersetzung: Inge Hanneforth
Farblithos: Litho Service T. Zamboni, Verona

Der Bereich Kunstbücher von BAYARD PRESSE SA

ISBN 2-87939-154-7
Deutsche Ausgabe: © 1998
Verlegernummer: 196
Printed in Italy

"I walked around all day, my mind occupied, seeking on the streets photographs to be taken directly from life as if in flagrante delicto. I wanted above all to seize in a single image the essence of any scene that cropped up. [...] Photography is the only means of expression which freezes one specific instant", wrote Henri Cartier-Bresson, one of the founding members of the Magnum Photos Agency.
During their assignments to the four corners of the earth, the photographers of this prestigious agency have all wanted to record a certain reality directly seized "from life" and to show the world as they saw and felt it. Their photographs bear witness to the experience of men, to places, times and events which their cameras have managed to capture. The personal imprint they leave on them proves, in the words of John Steinbeck, that "the camera need not be a cold mechanical device. Like the pen, it is as good as the man who uses it. It can be the extension of mind and heart...".
The ambition of the series to which this album belongs is to recall the finest of these "decisive moments", where the eye of the photographer encounters the diversity of the world. Whether it is read like a report or looked at like a film, each album is above all a thematic, historic and aesthetic odyssey bringing together the best pictures from the Magnum photographers.

« JE marchais toute la journée, l'esprit tendu, cherchant dans les rues à prendre sur le vif des photos comme des flagrants délits. J'avais surtout le désir de saisir dans une seule image l'essentiel d'une scène qui surgissait. [...] De tous les moyens d'expression, la photo est le seul qui fixe un instant précis », écrivait Henri Cartier-Bresson, l'un des fondateurs de l'agence Magnum Photos.
Les photographes de cette prestigieuse agence ont tous voulu, au cours de leurs reportages à travers le monde, rendre compte d'une certaine réalité « sur le vif » et montrer le monde tel qu'ils le voyaient et le ressentaient. Leurs photos témoignent de l'expérience d'hommes, de lieux, d'époques et d'événements que leur appareil a su capter. L' empreinte personnelle qu'ils laissent prouve, selon les mots de John Steinbeck, que « l'appareil-photo n'est pas nécessairement une froide mécanique. Comme la plume pour l'écrivain, tout dépend de qui la manie. Il peut être un prolongement de l'esprit et du cœur... »
Restituer les plus beaux de ces « instants décisifs » au fil desquels l'œil du photographe rencontre la diversité du monde, telle est l'ambition de la collection dans laquelle s'inscrit ce livre. À lire comme un récit ou à regarder comme un film, il est avant tout une promenade thématique, historique et esthétique qui rassemble les meilleurs clichés des photographes de Magnum Photos.

„DEN ganzen Tag lief ich angespannt herum, denn ich wollte in den Straßen wie auf frischer Tat ertappte, lebensnahe Fotos machen. Vor allem hatte ich den Wunsch, in einem einzigen Bild das Wesentliche eines Geschehnisses festzuhalten [...] Von allen Ausdrucksmitteln ist die Fotografie das einzige, das einen bestimmten Augenblick fixiert", schrieb Henri Cartier-Bresson, einer der Gründer der Fotoagentur Agence Magnum Photos.
Den Fotografen dieser renommierten Agentur liegt viel daran, auf ihren Reportagen in aller Welt von einer gewissen „lebensnahen" Realität Zeugnis abzulegen und die Welt so zu zeigen, wie sie sie sahen und empfanden. Die Fotos sind von ihrem Apparat eingefangene Erfahrungen mit Menschen, Orten, Zeiten und Ereignissen. Der persönliche Eindruck, die sie hinterlassen, beweist, um mit Steinbeck zu sprechen, daß „der Fotoapparat keine kalte Mechanik sein muß. Wie bei der Feder des Schriftstellers hängt alles davon ab, wer sie hält. Und manchmal ist es sogar eine Verlängerung von Geist und Gefühl ..." Die schönsten dieser „entscheidenen Augenblicke" zu zeigen, bei denen das Auge des Fotografen der Vielfältigkeit der Welt begegnet, ist die Absicht dieser Buchreihe. Wie ein Bericht zu lesen oder wie ein Film zu betrachten, ist sie vor allem ein thematischer, historischer und ästhetischer Spaziergang, auf dem die besten Bilder der Fotografen von Magnum Photos zu sehen sind.

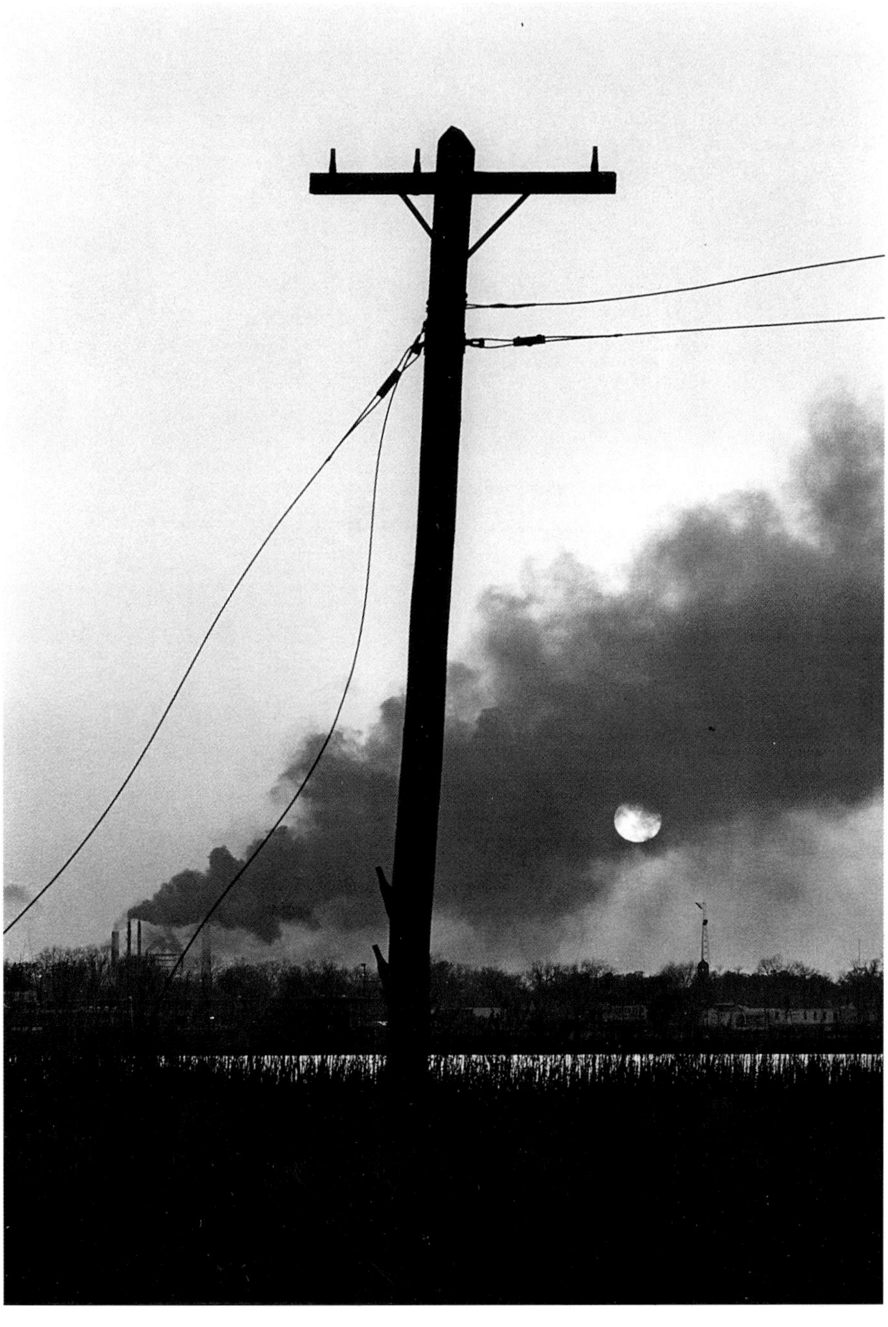

Hiroshi Hamaya, USA, *États-Unis,* 1964.

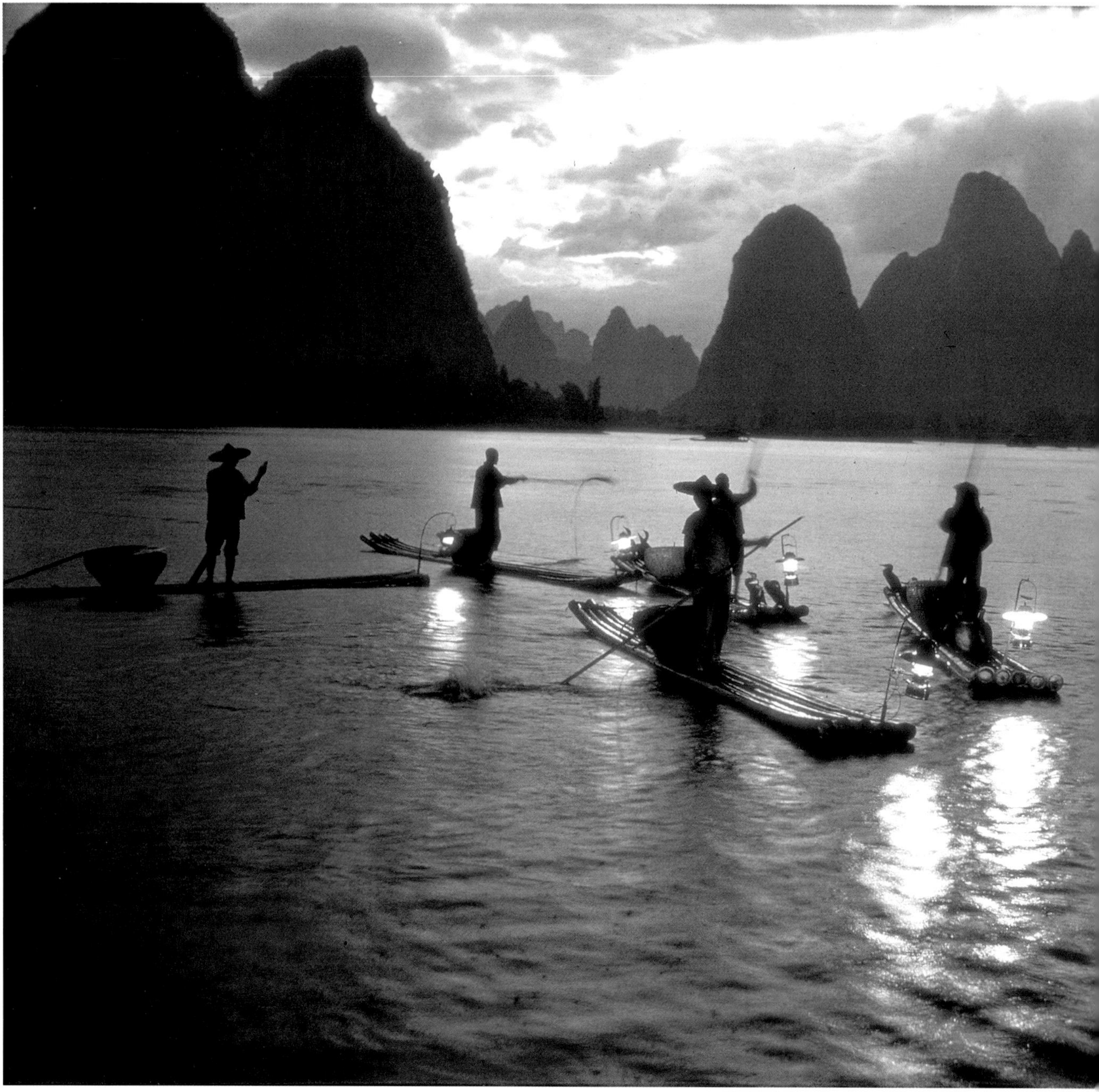

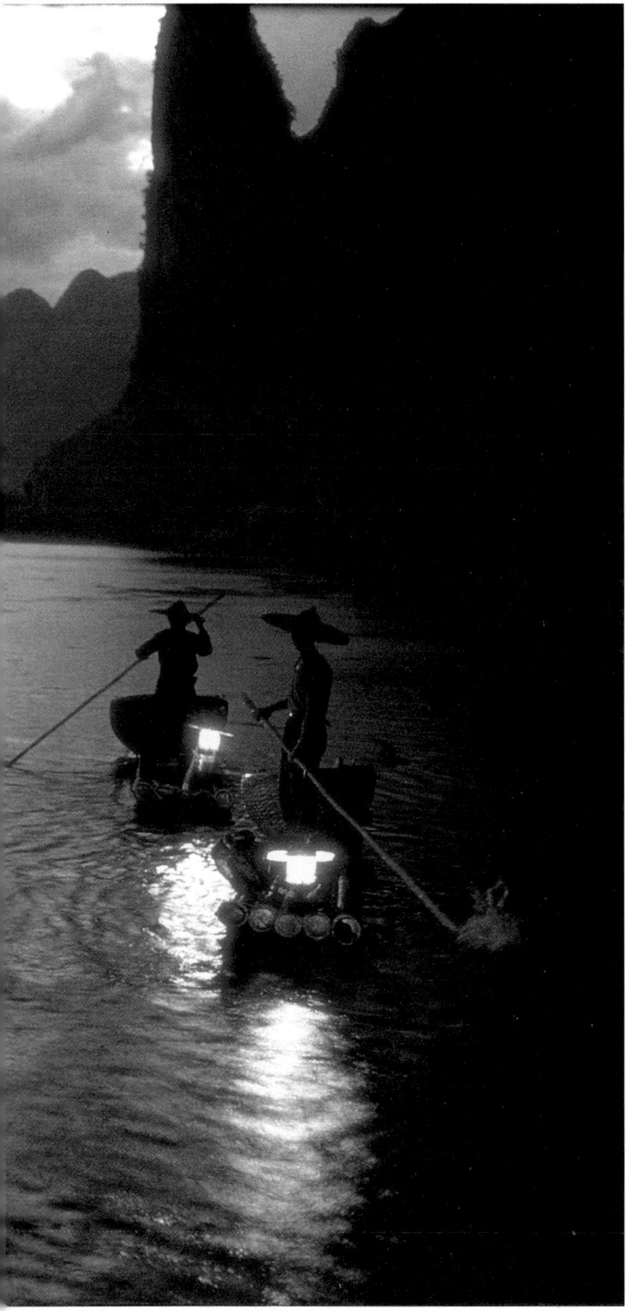

Hiroji Kubota, China, *Chine,* 1985.

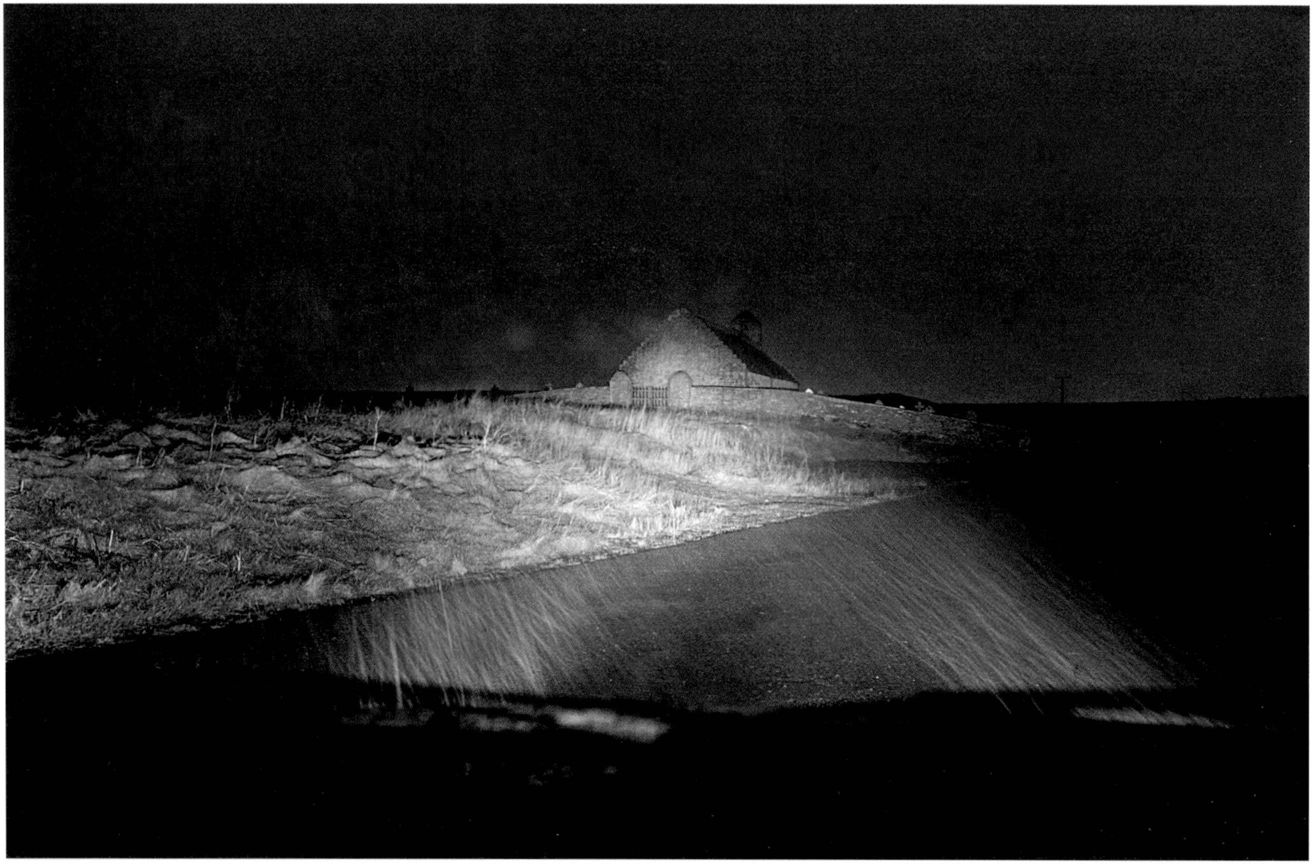

 Peter Marlow, Scotland, *Écosse,* Schottland, 1994.

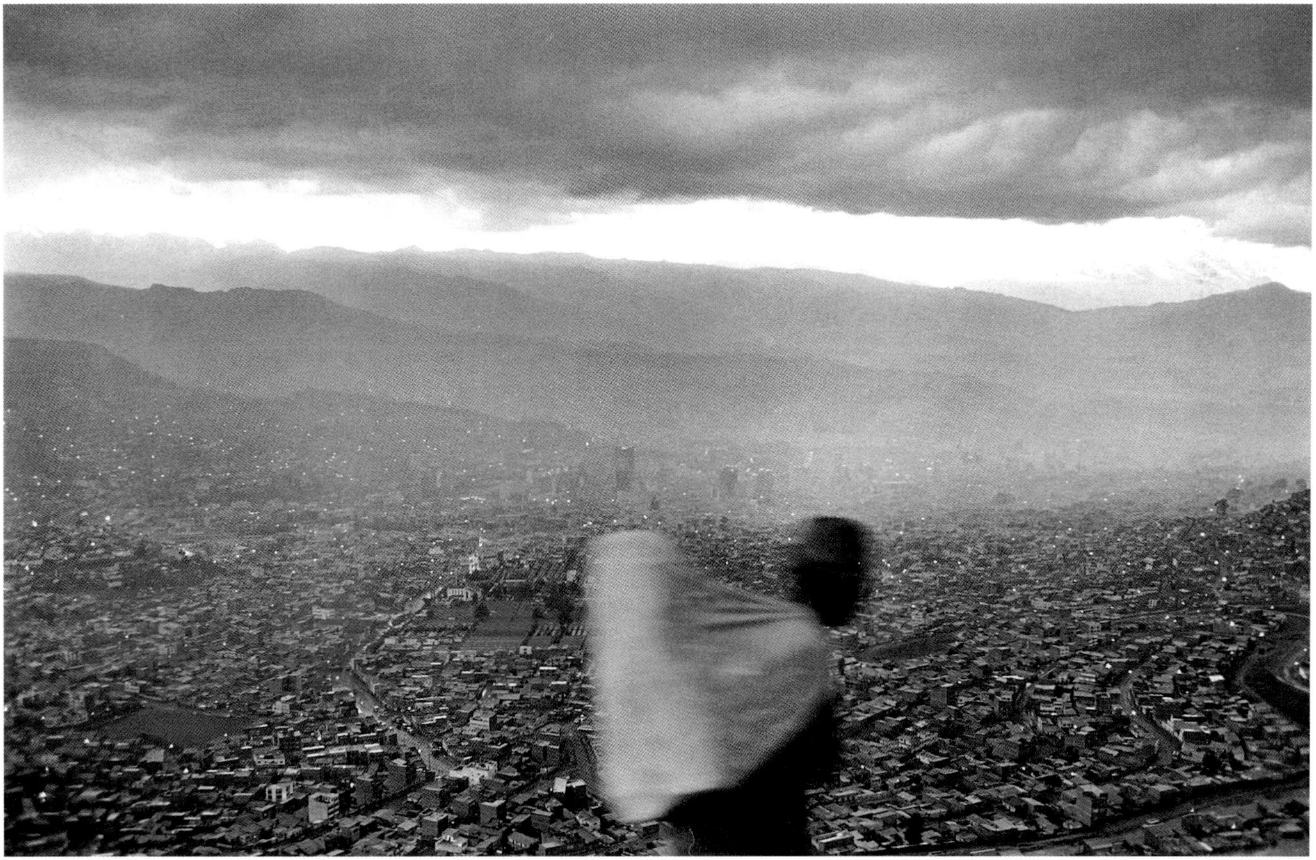

Chris Steele-Perkins, Bolivia, *Bolivie,* Bolivien, 1984.

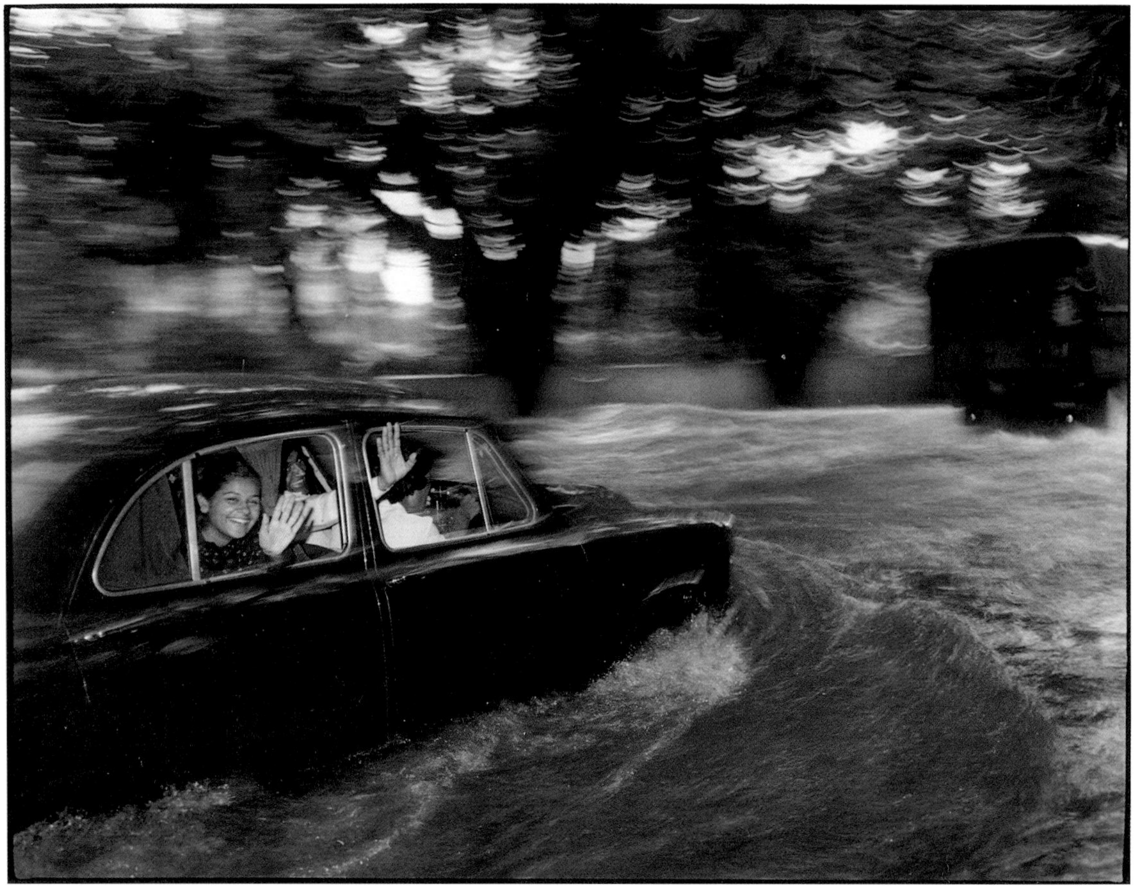

 Carl De Keyzer, India, *Inde,* Indien, 1985.

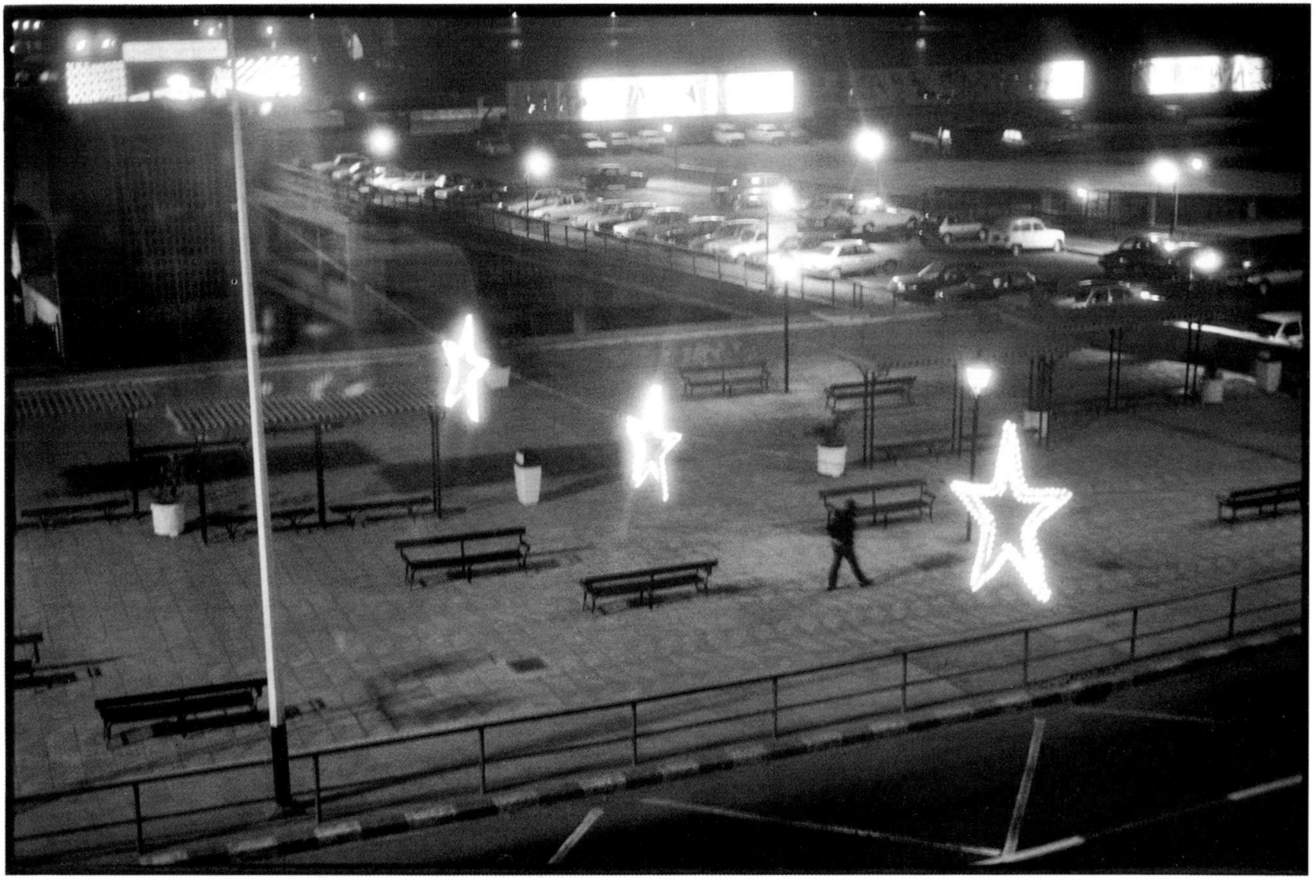

Raymond Depardon, Algeria, *Algérie,* Algerien, 1986.

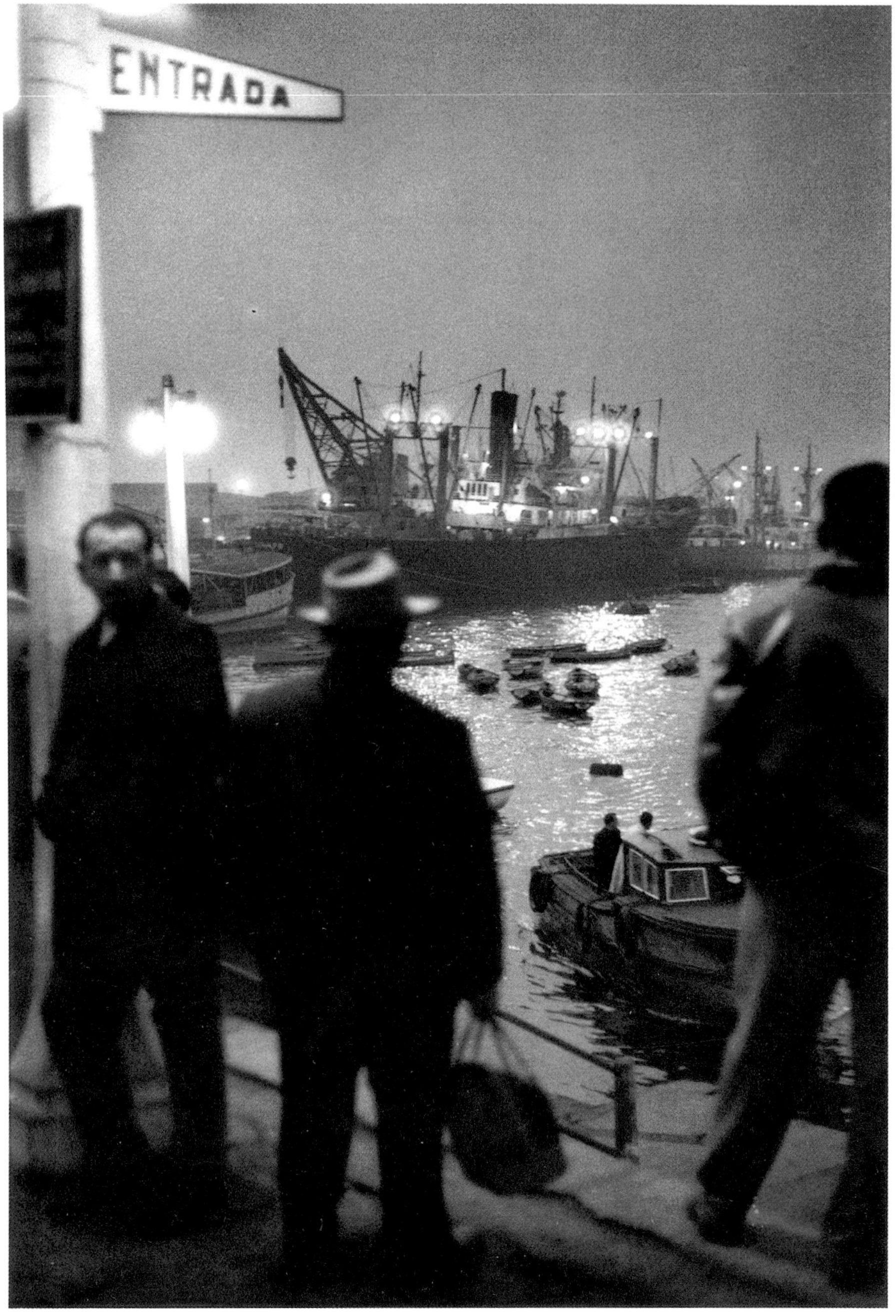

 Sergio Larrain, Chile, *Chili,* 1963.

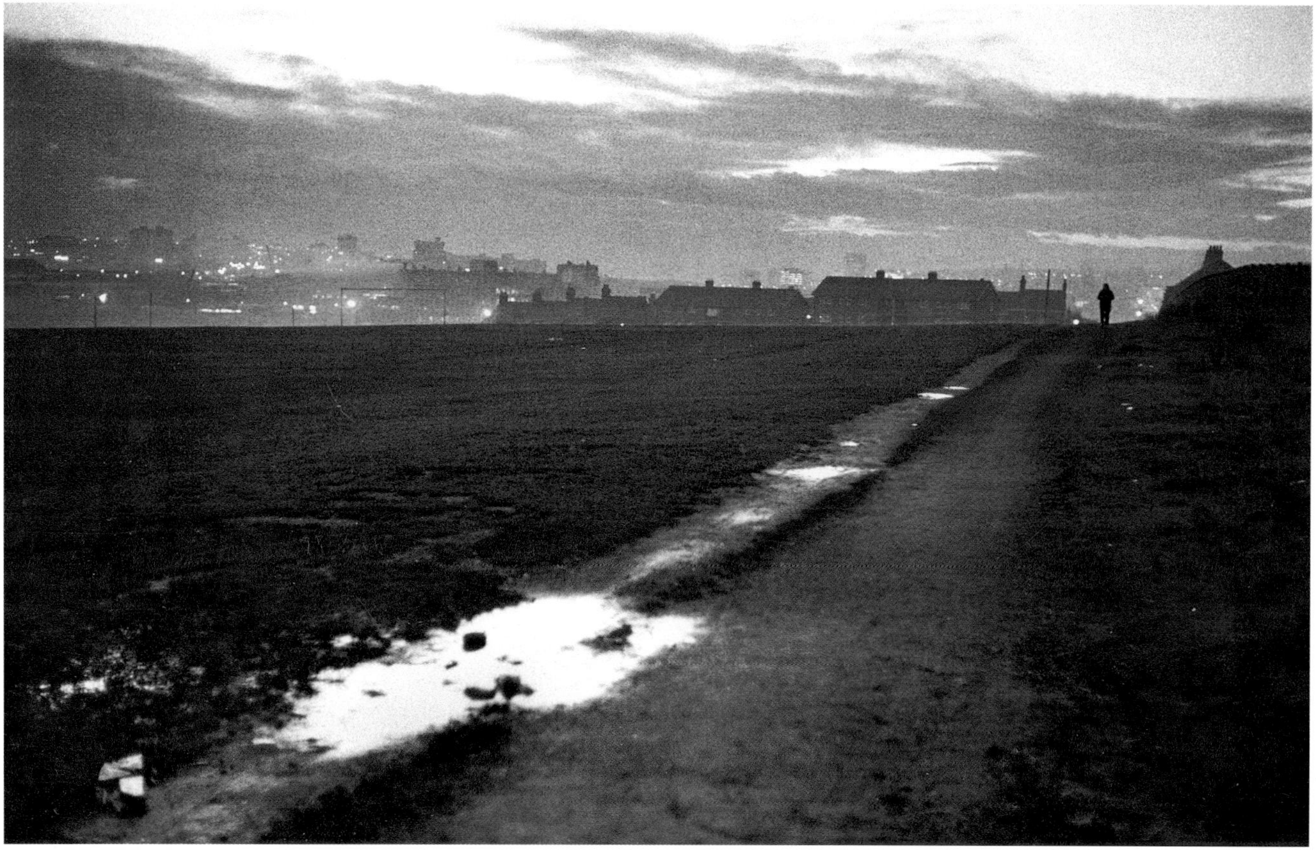

Ian Berry, England, *Angleterre,* 1974.

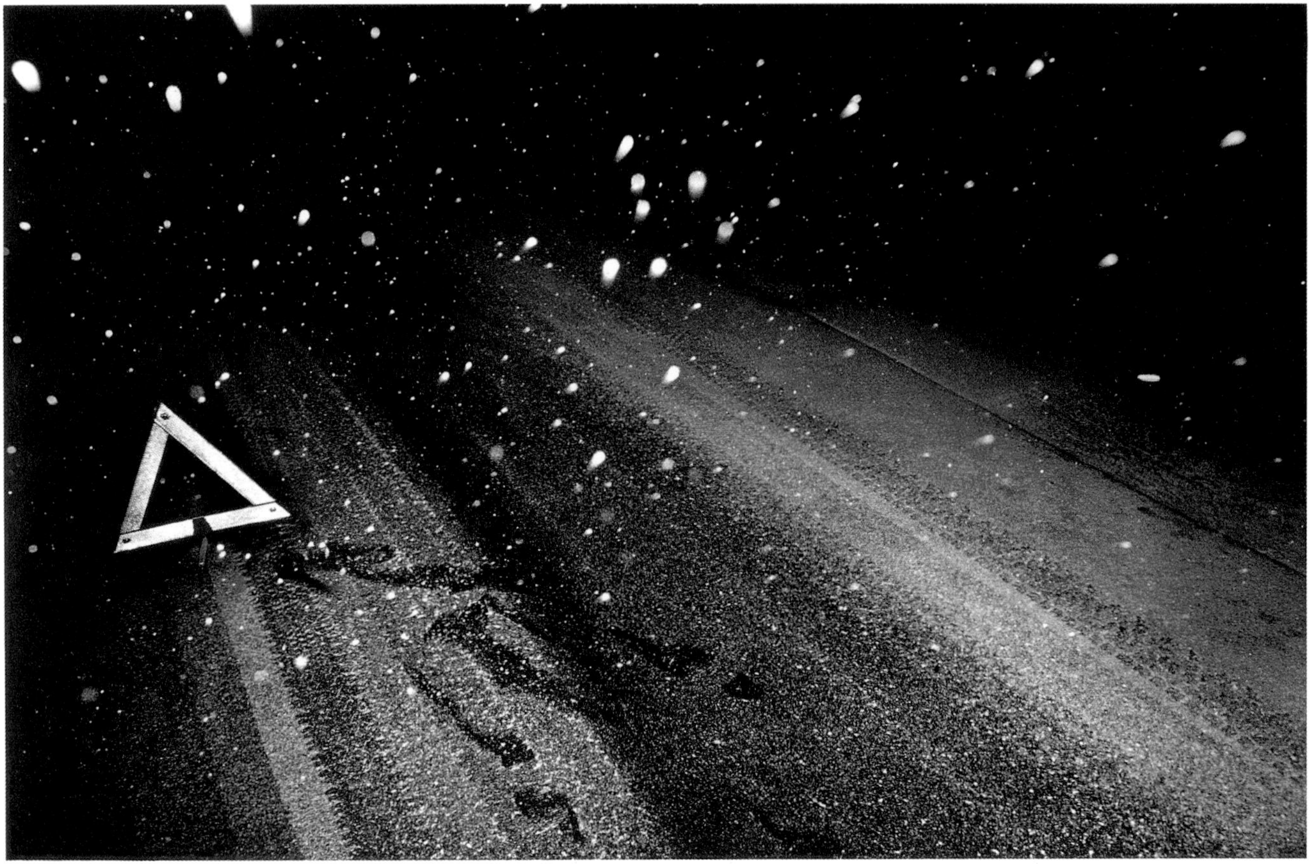

 Josef Koudelka, Switzerland, *Suisse,* Schweiz, 1978.

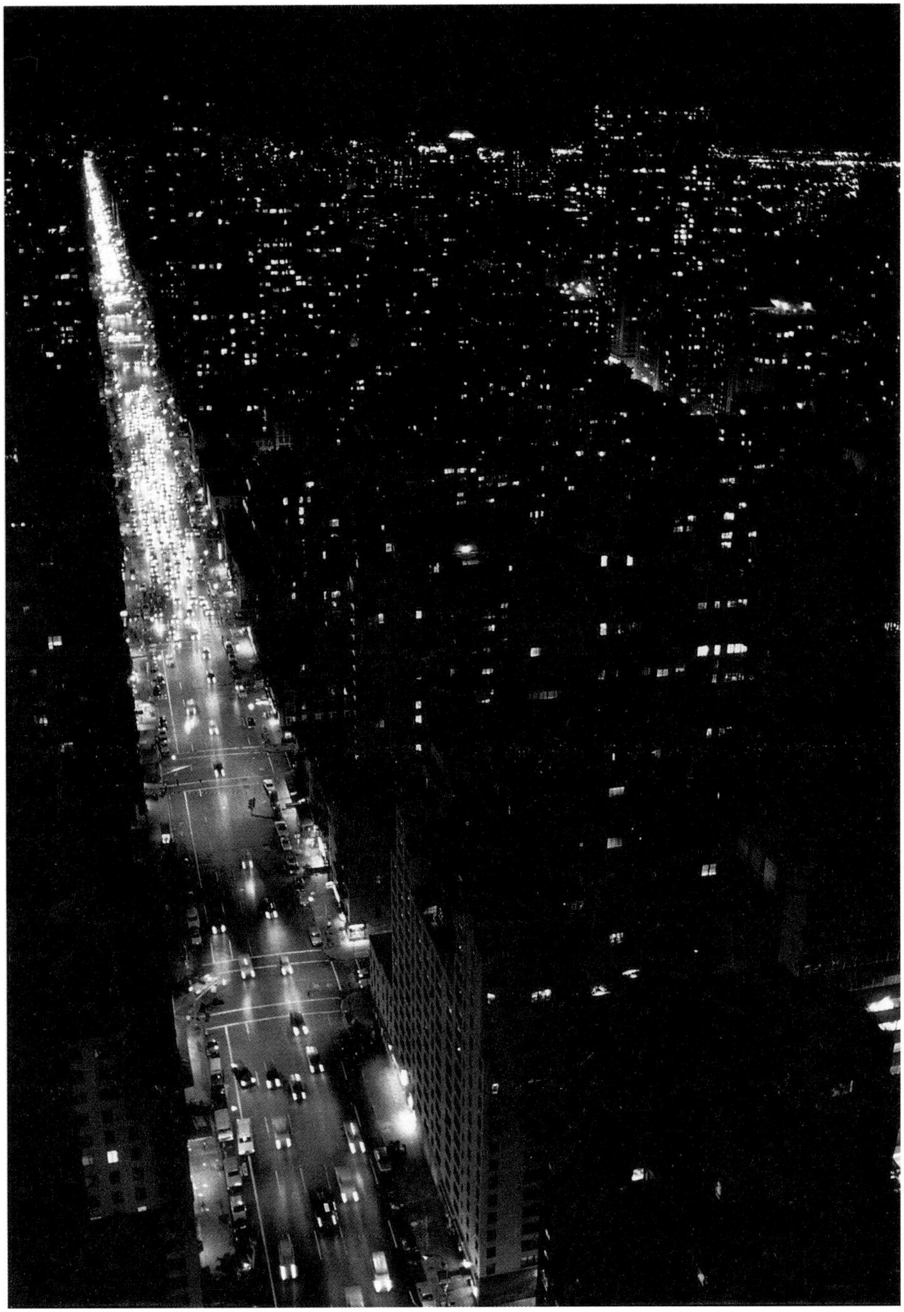

Ferdinando Scianna, USA, *États-Unis,* 1985.

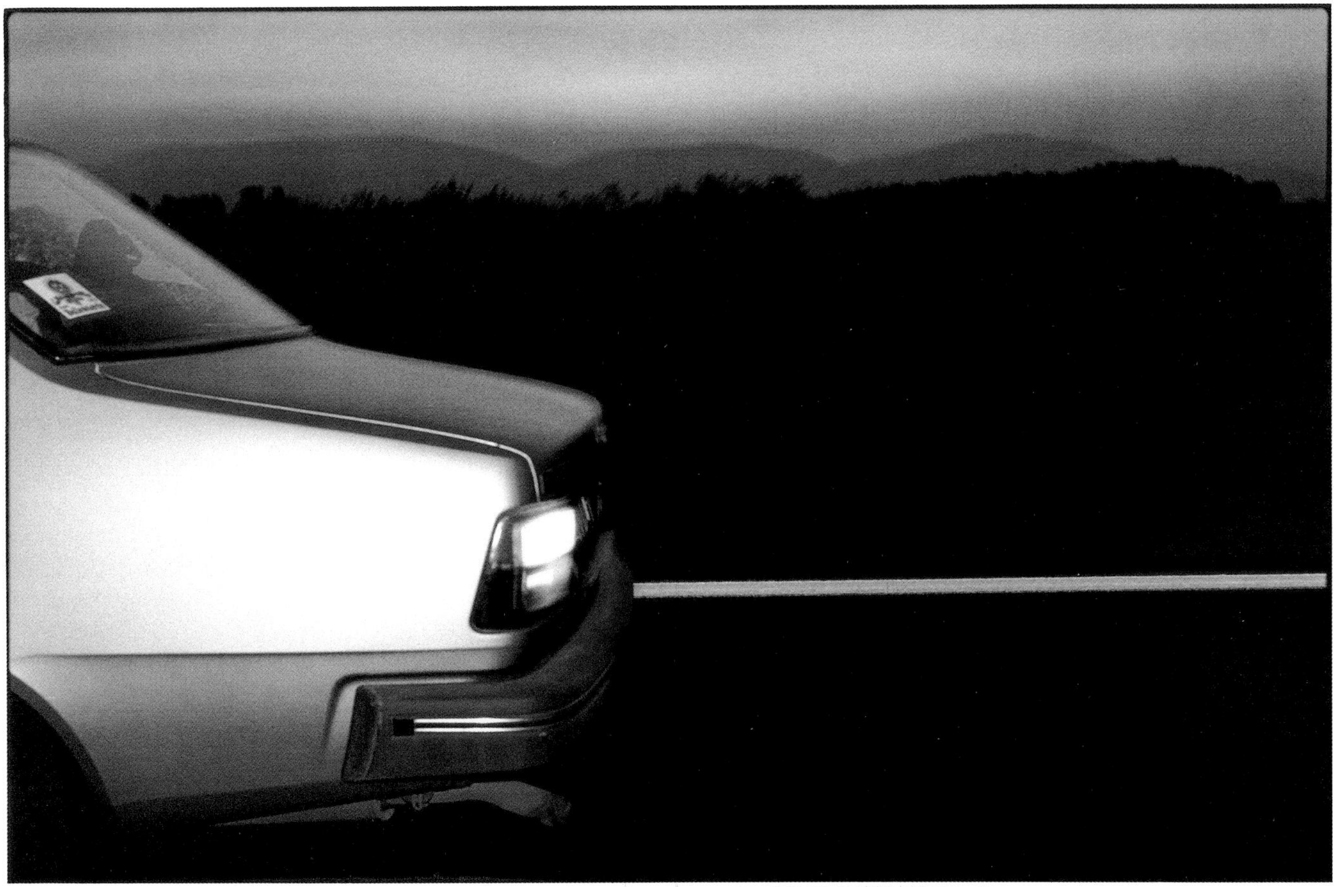

Patrick Zachmann, *France,* Frankreich, 1983.

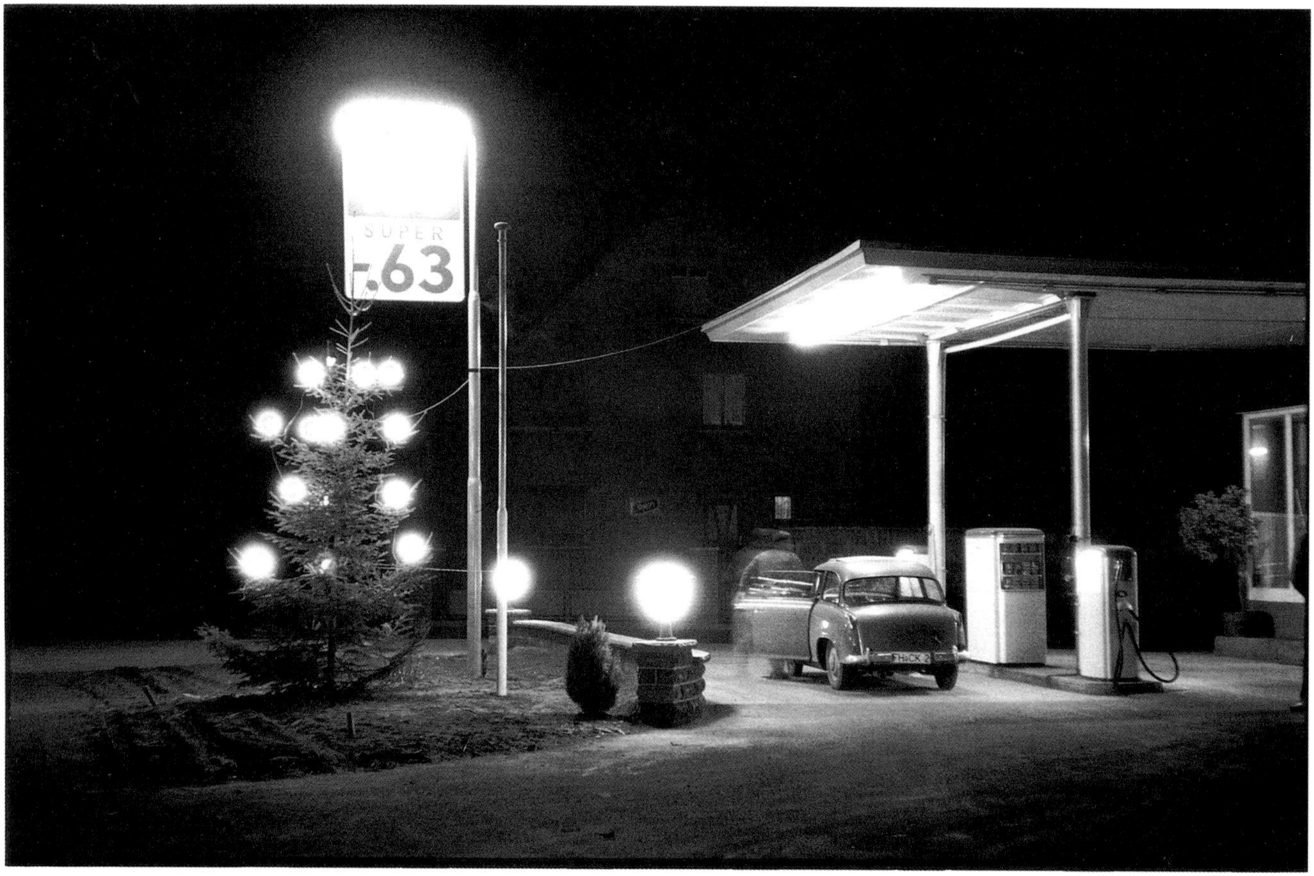

 René Burri, Federal Republic of Germany, *RFA,* Bundesrepublik Deutschland, 1960.

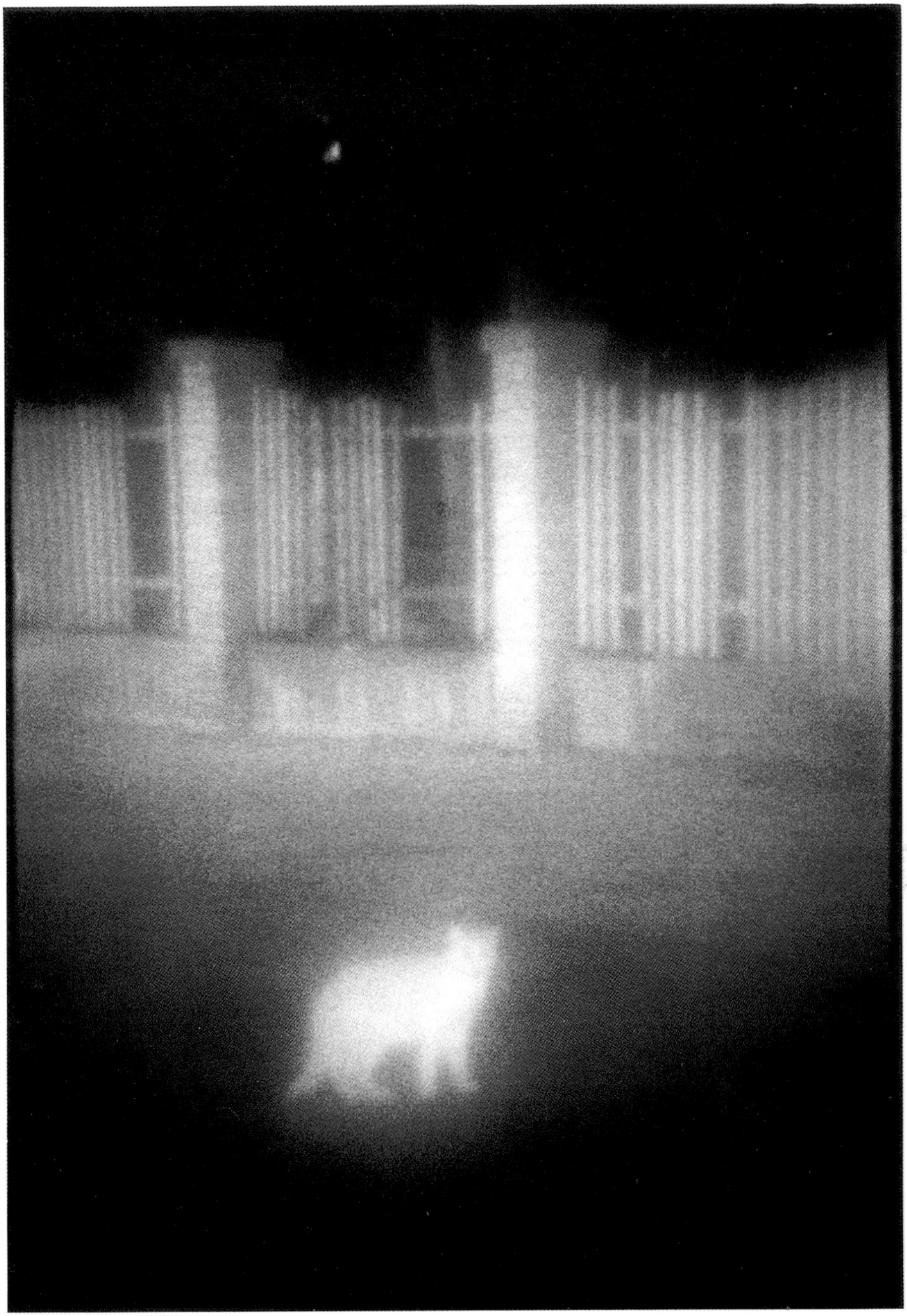

Luc Delahaye, Italy, *Italie,* Italien, 1992.

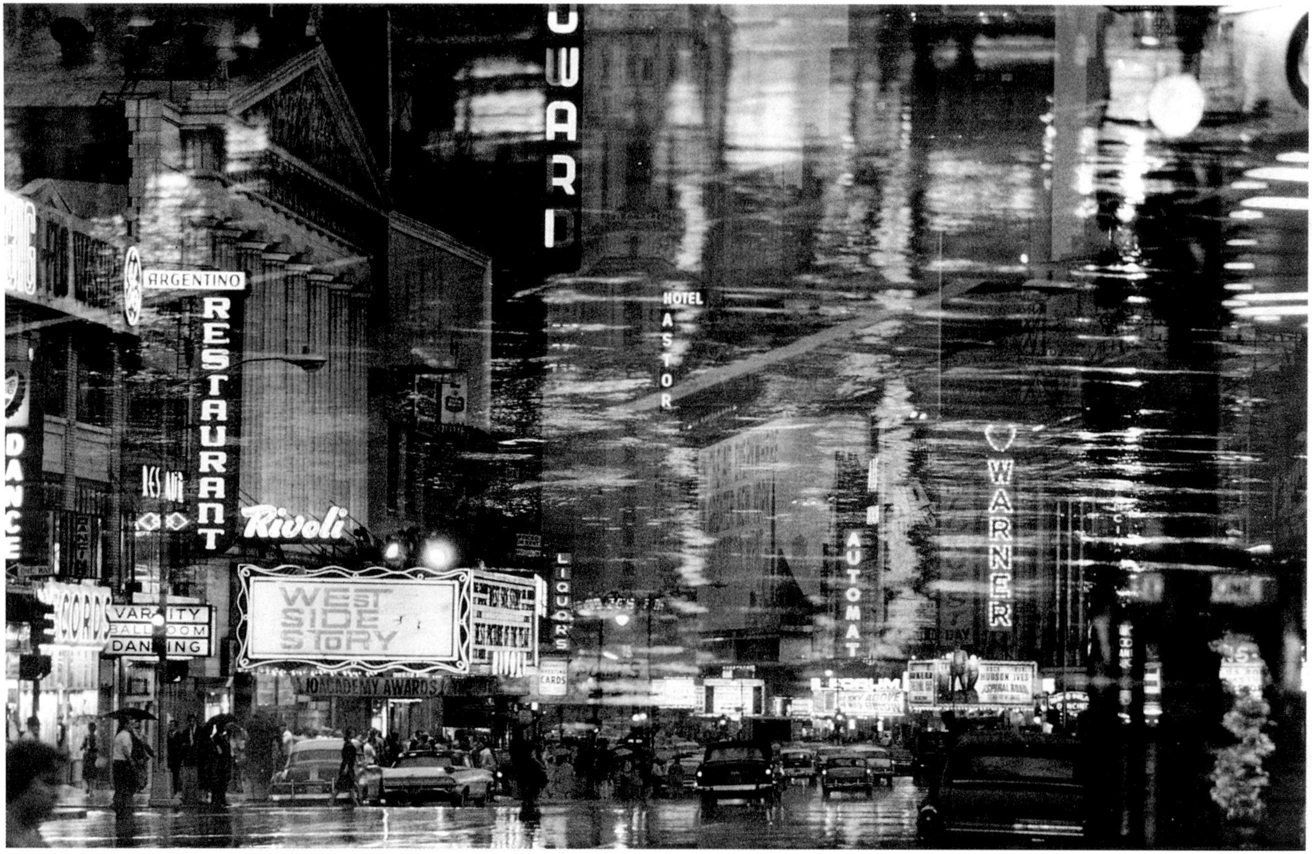

 Ernst Haas, USA, *États-Unis,* 1962.

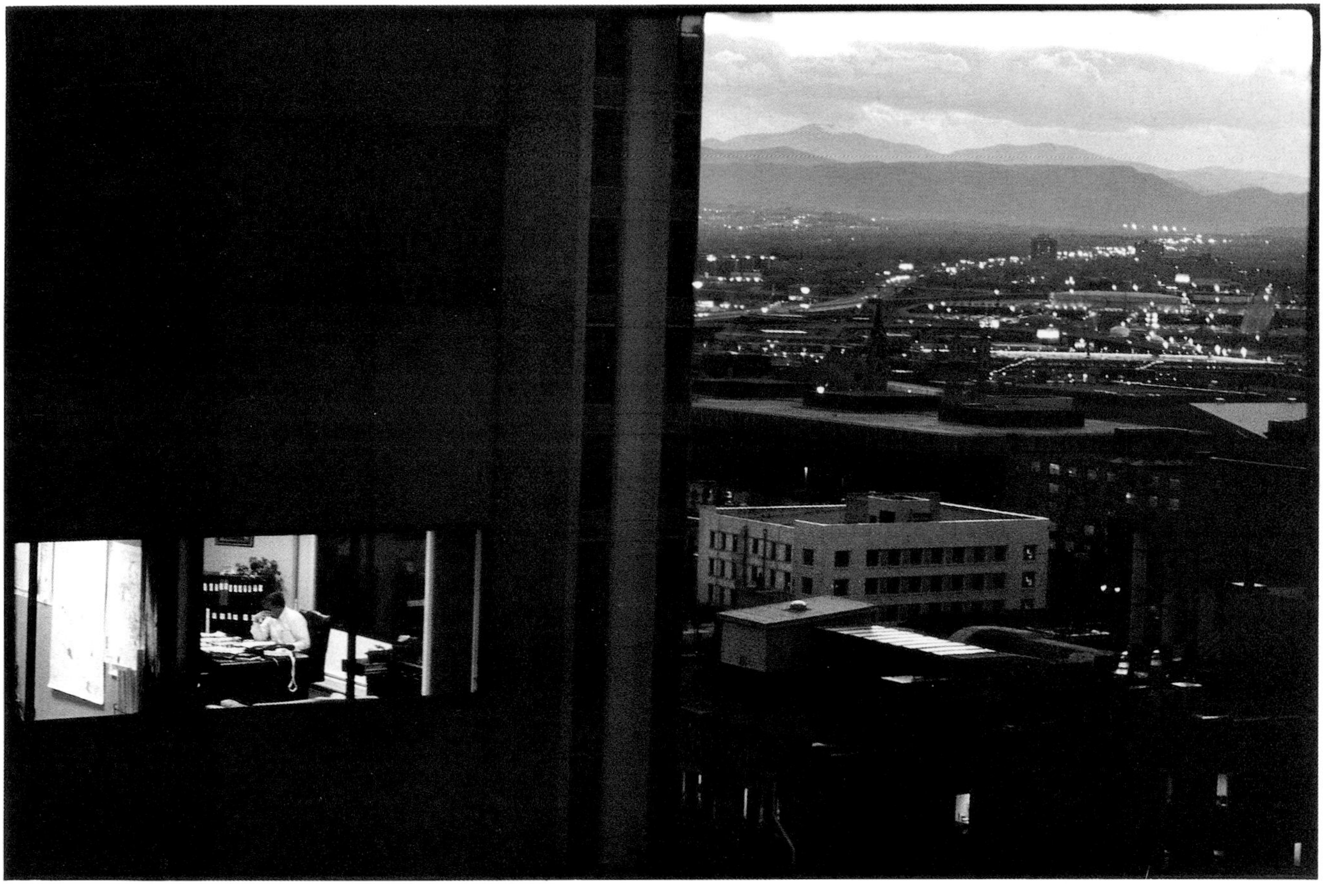

René Burri, USA, *États-Unis*, 1992.

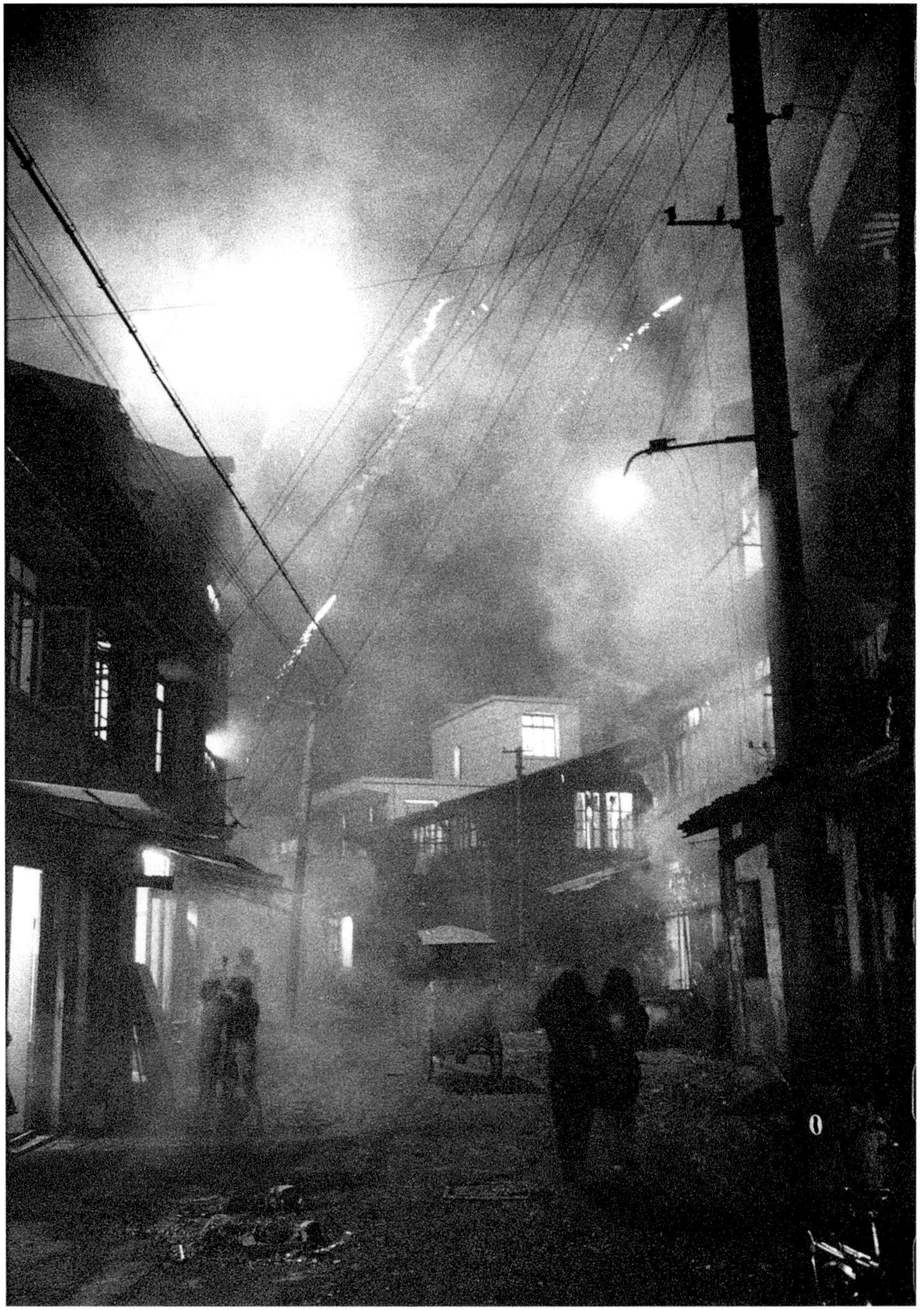

Patrick Zachmann, China, *Chine,* 1991.

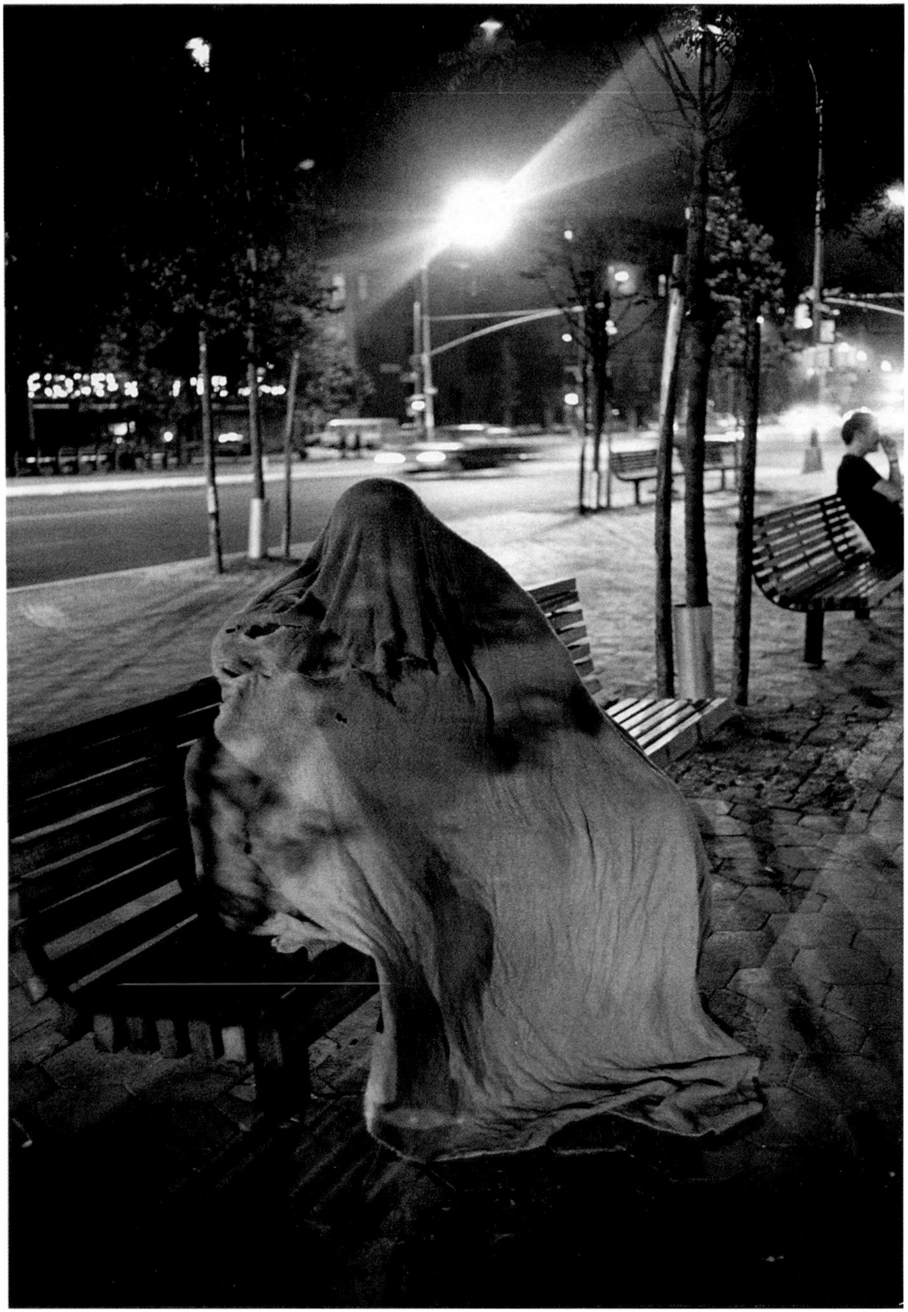

24 Gilles Peress, USA, *États-Unis,* 1975.

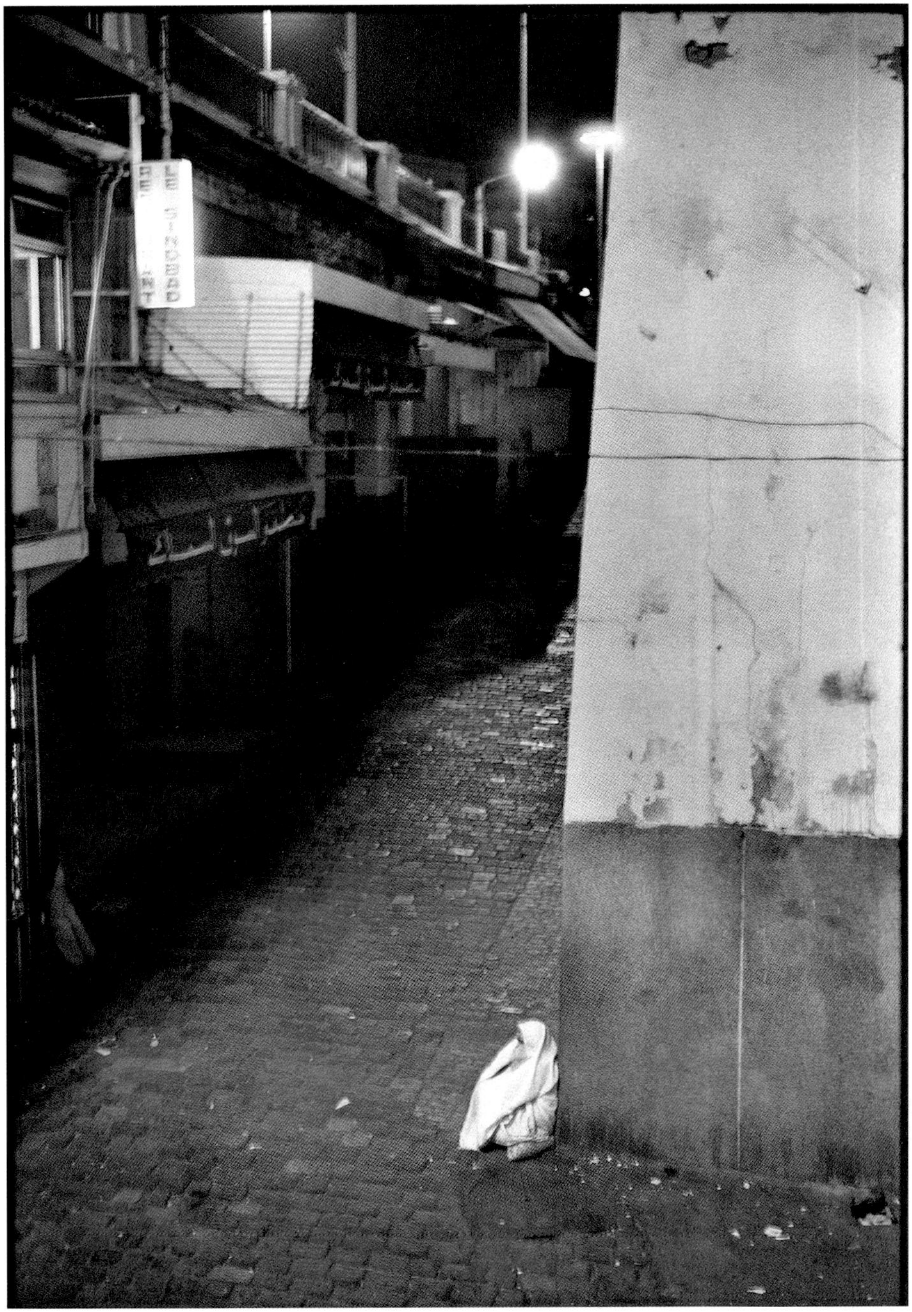

Abbas, Algeria, *Algérie,* Algerien, 1982.

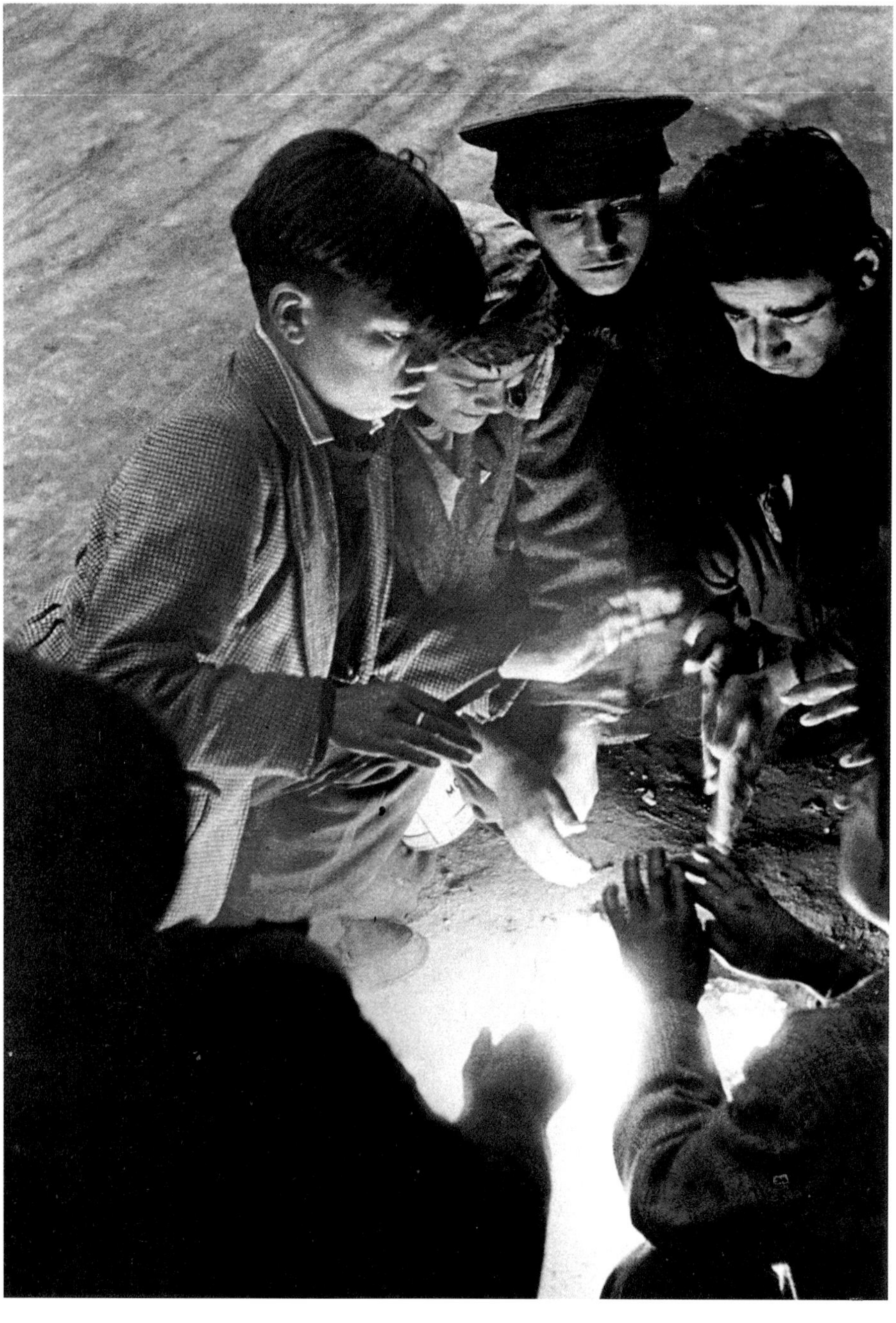

 Sergio Larrain, Chile, *Chili,* 1957.

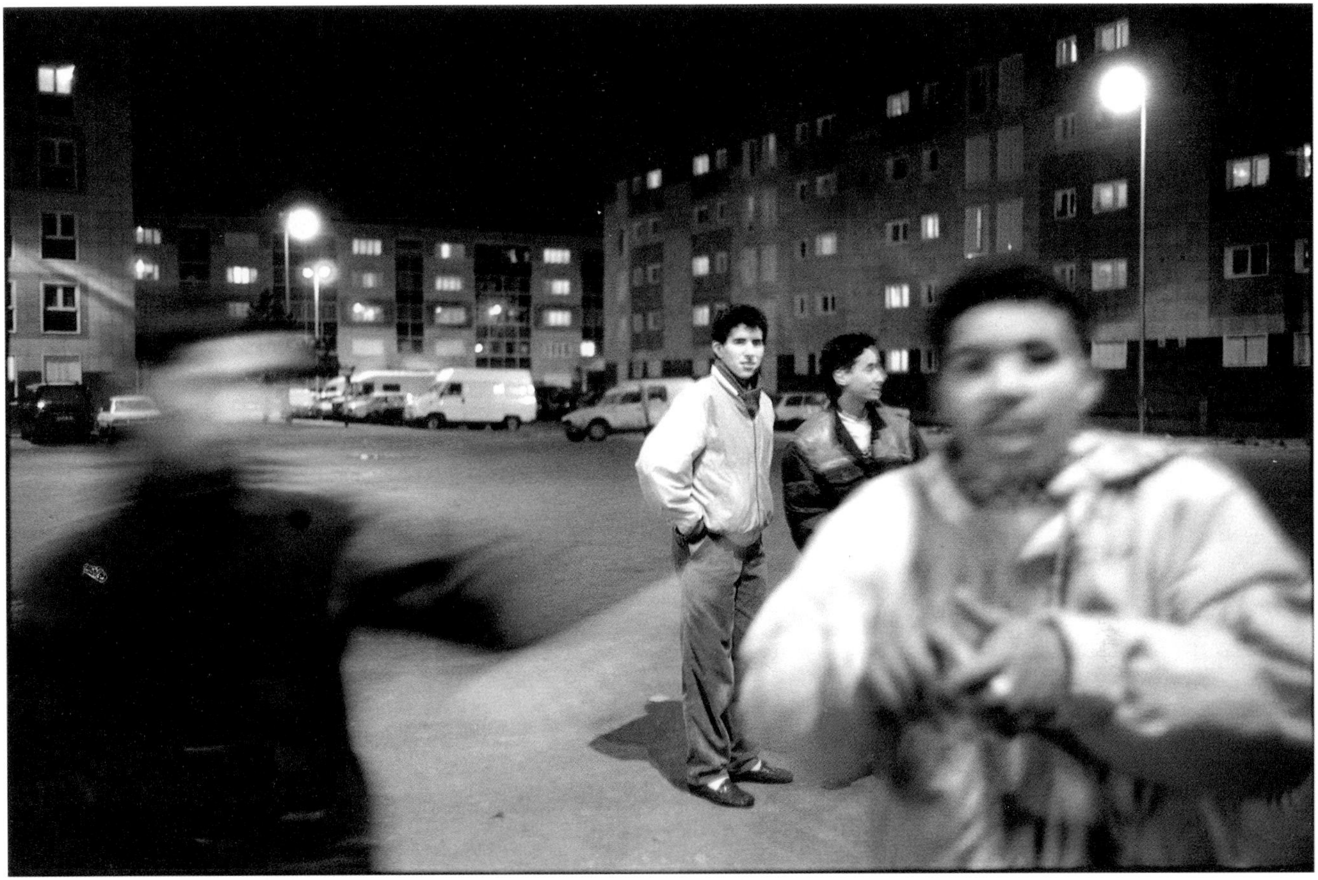

Patrick Zachmann, *France,* Frankreich, 1990.

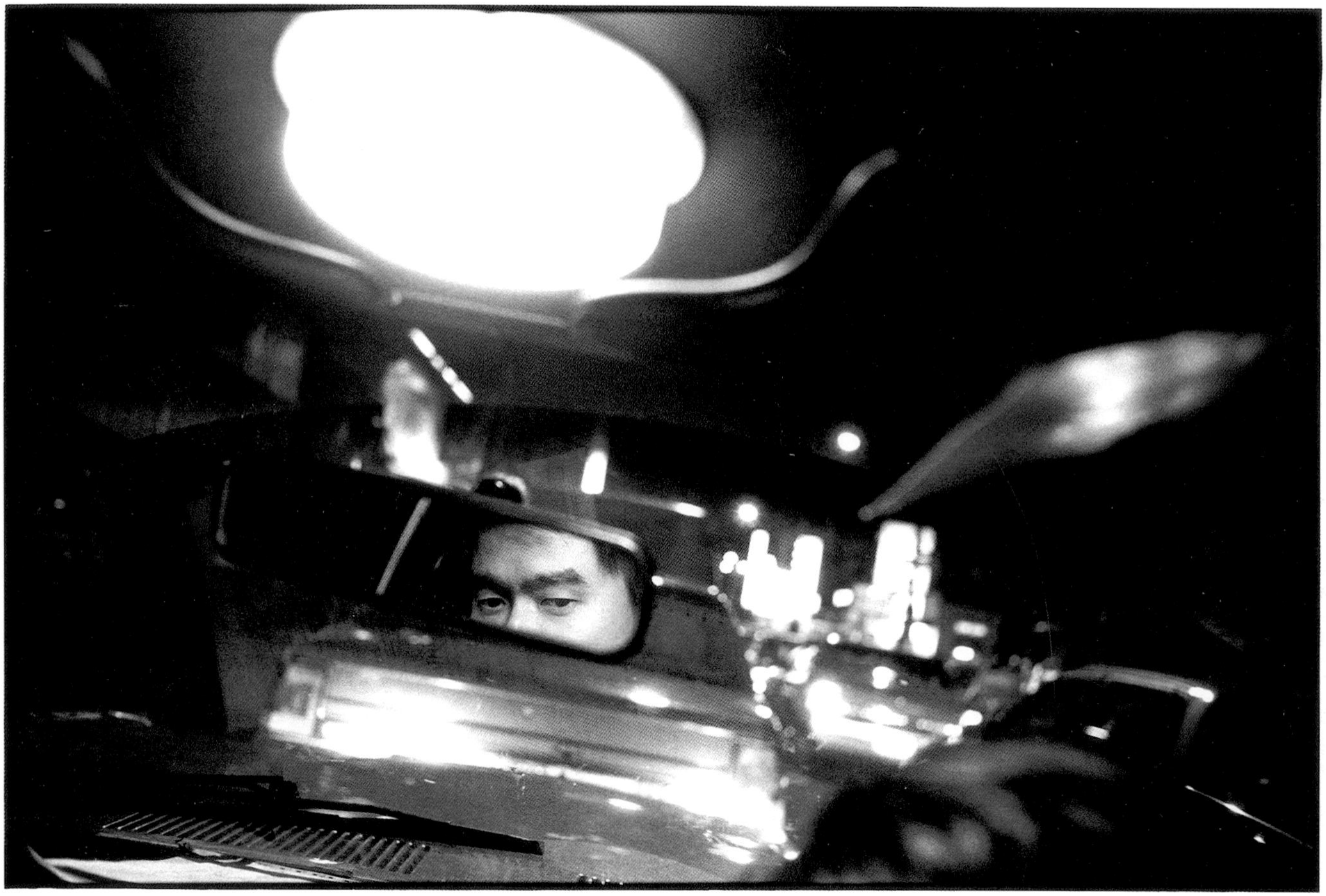

 Patrick Zachmann, USA, *États-Unis,* 1987.

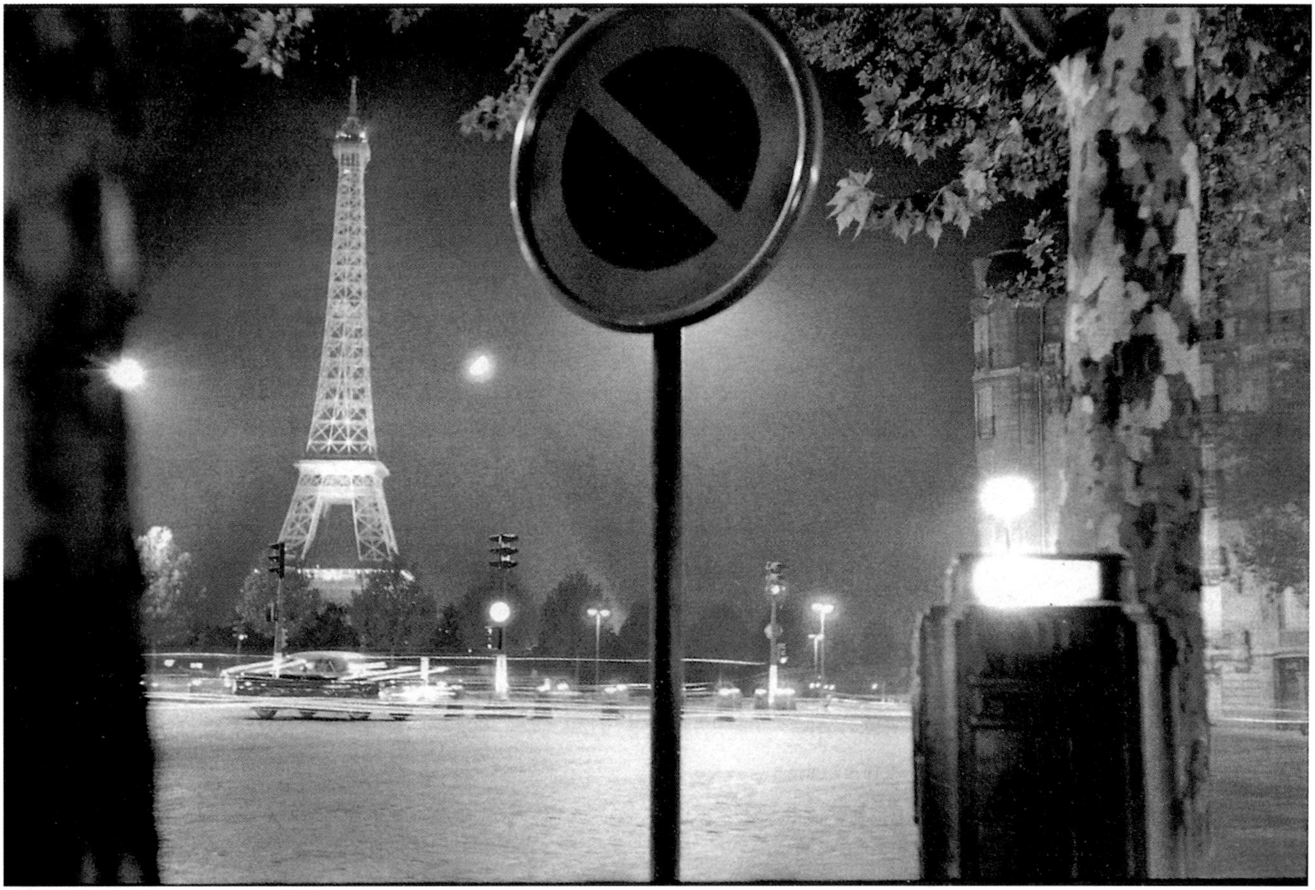

René Burri, *France,* Frankreich, 1962.

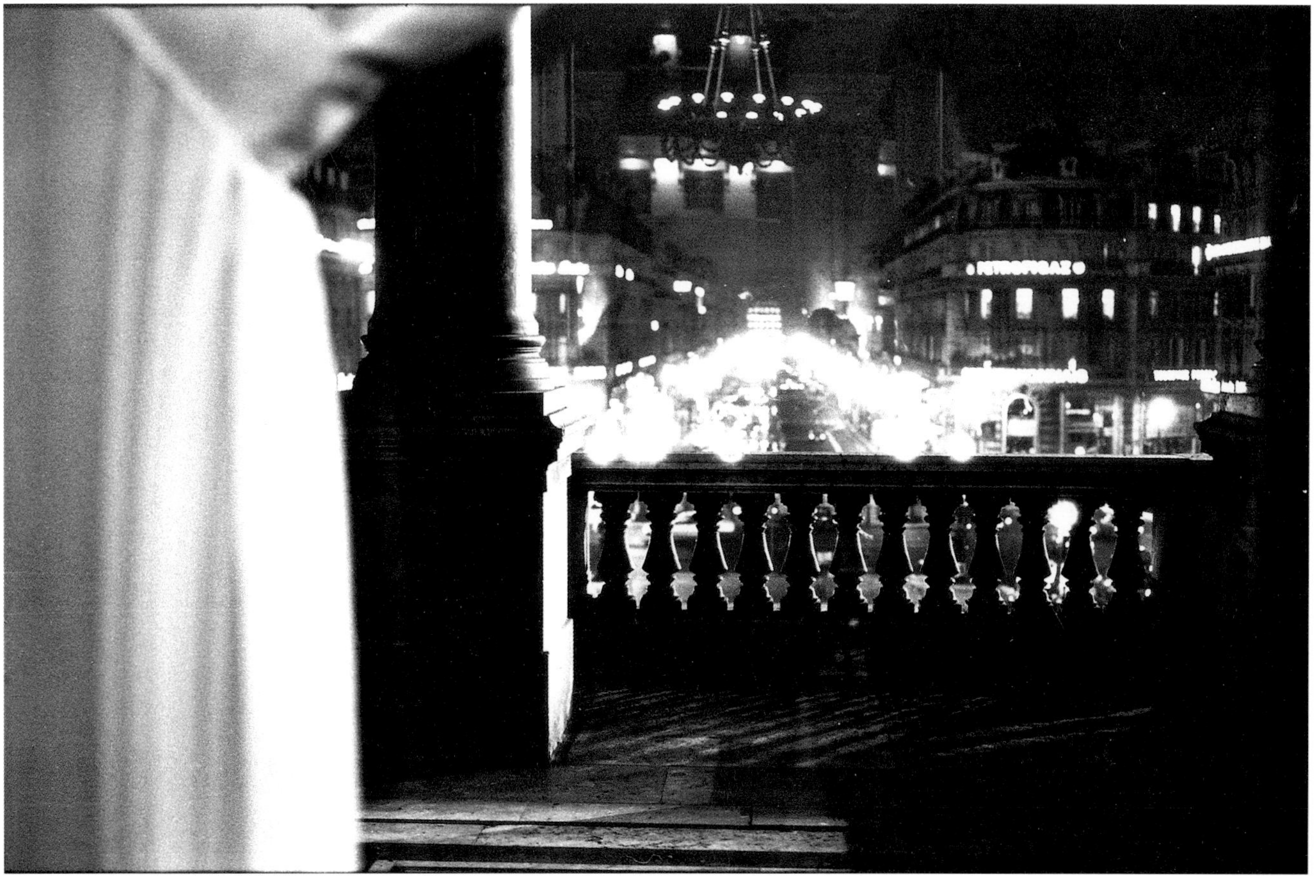

Raymond Depardon, *France*, Frankreich, 1985.

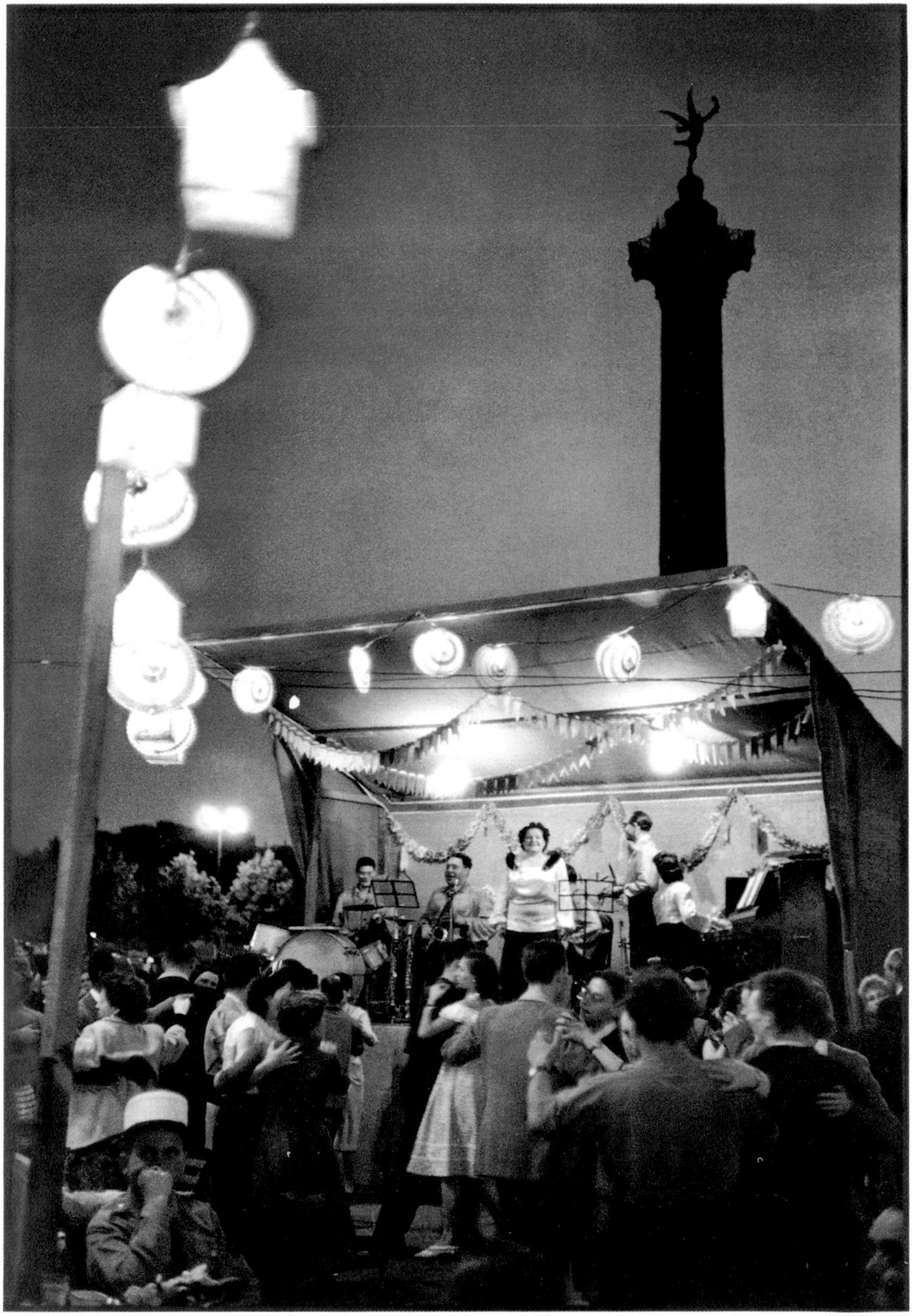

32 | Henri Cartier-Bresson, *France,* Frankreich, 1952.

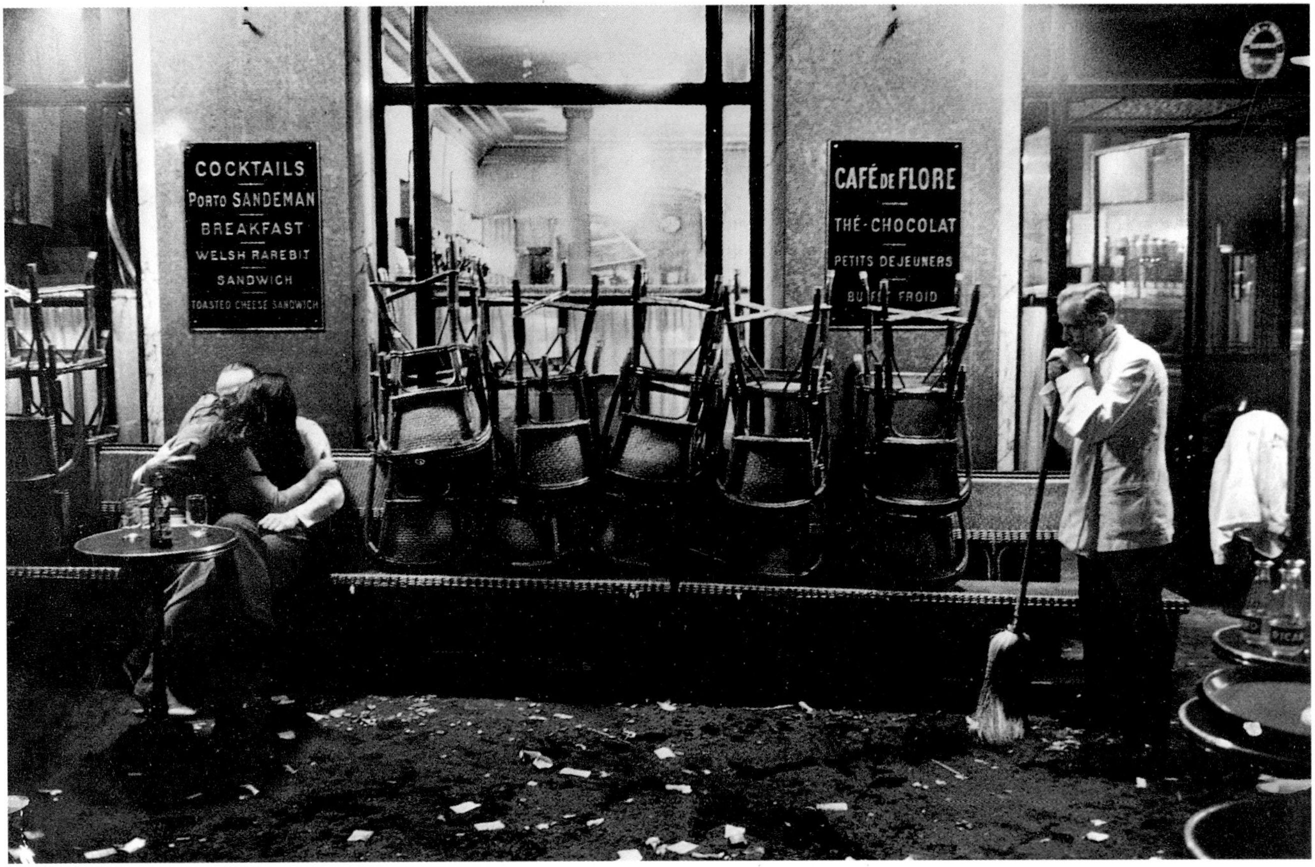

Dennis Stock, *France,* Frankreich, 1958.

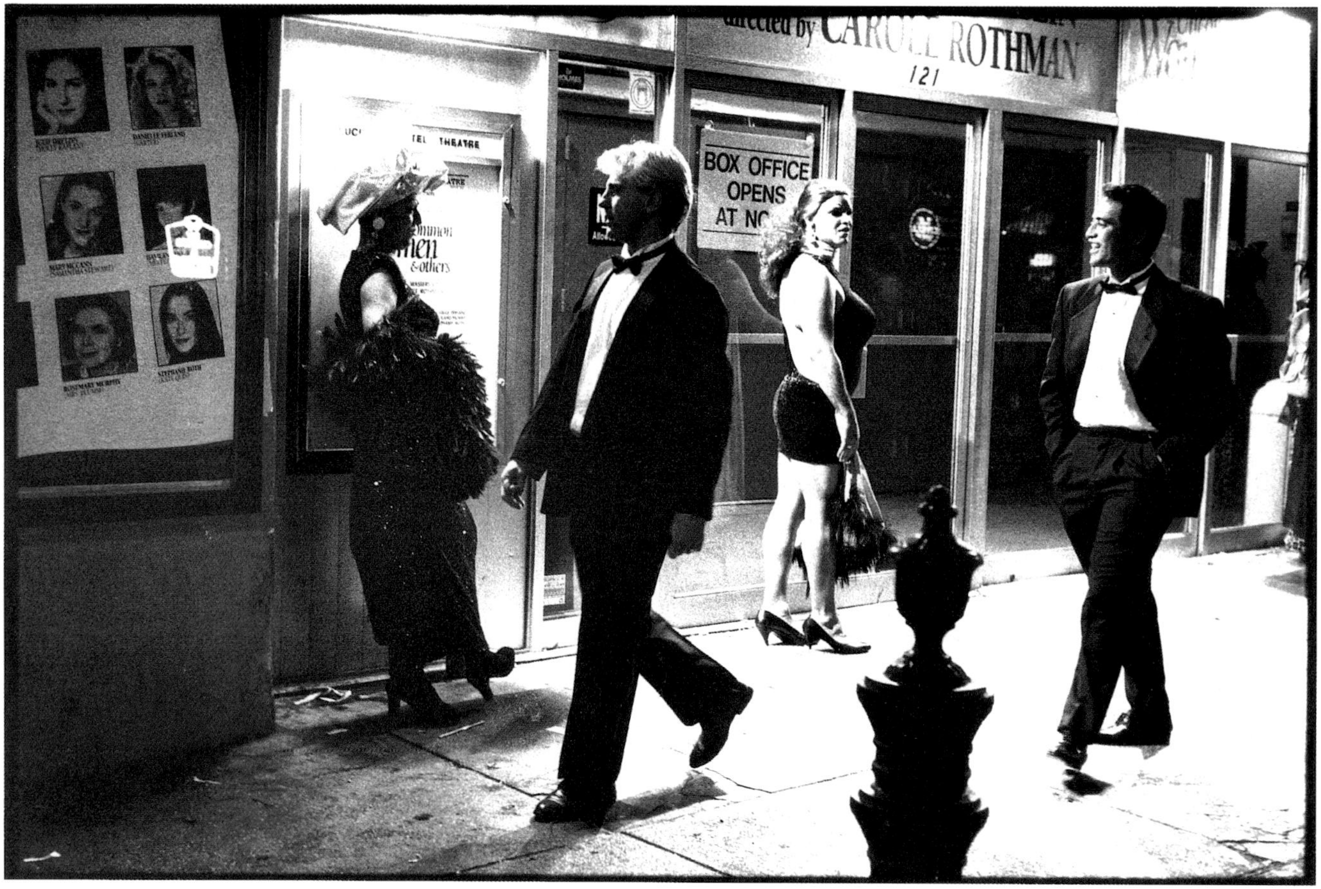

 Leonard Freed, USA, *États-Unis,* 1995.

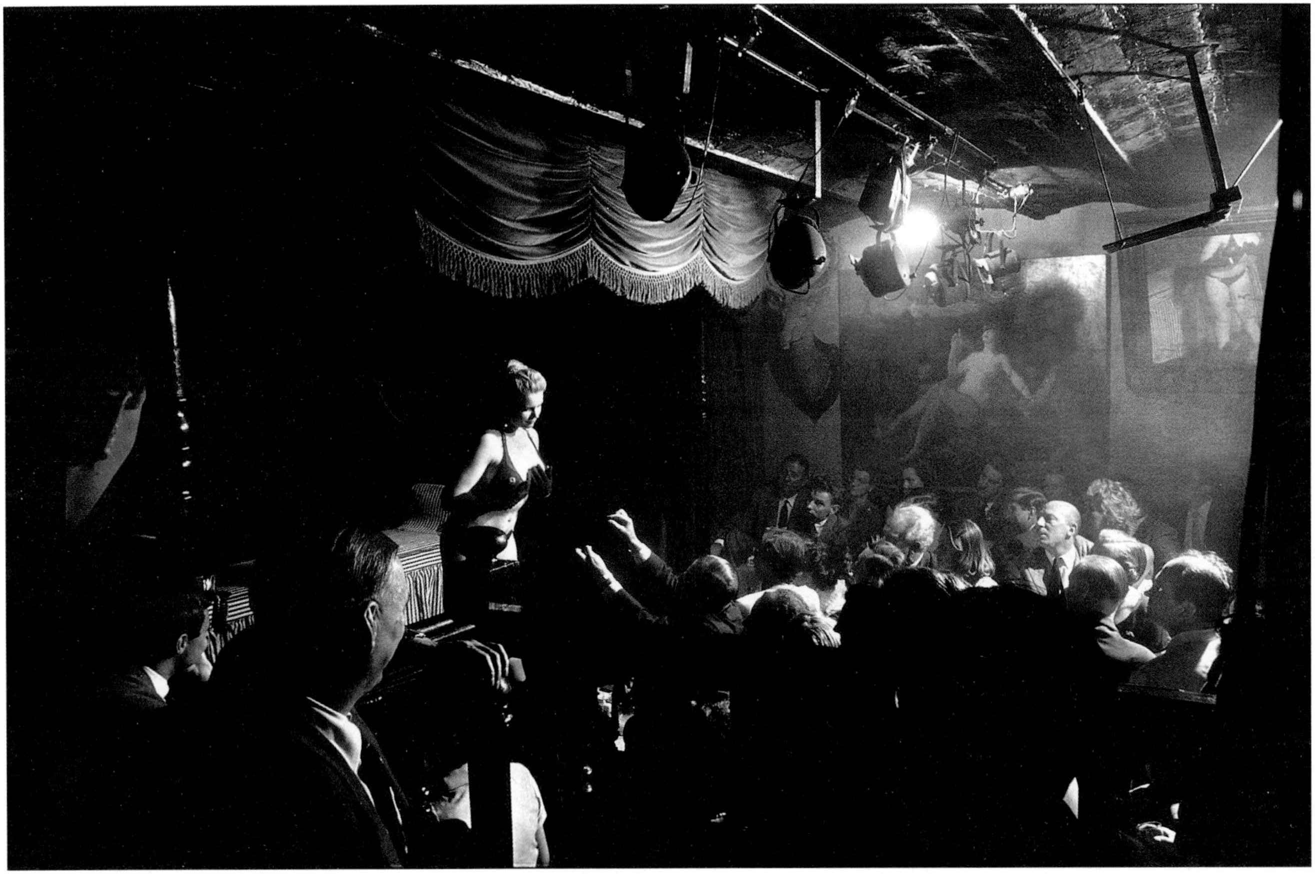

Burt Glinn, *France,* Frankreich, 1956.

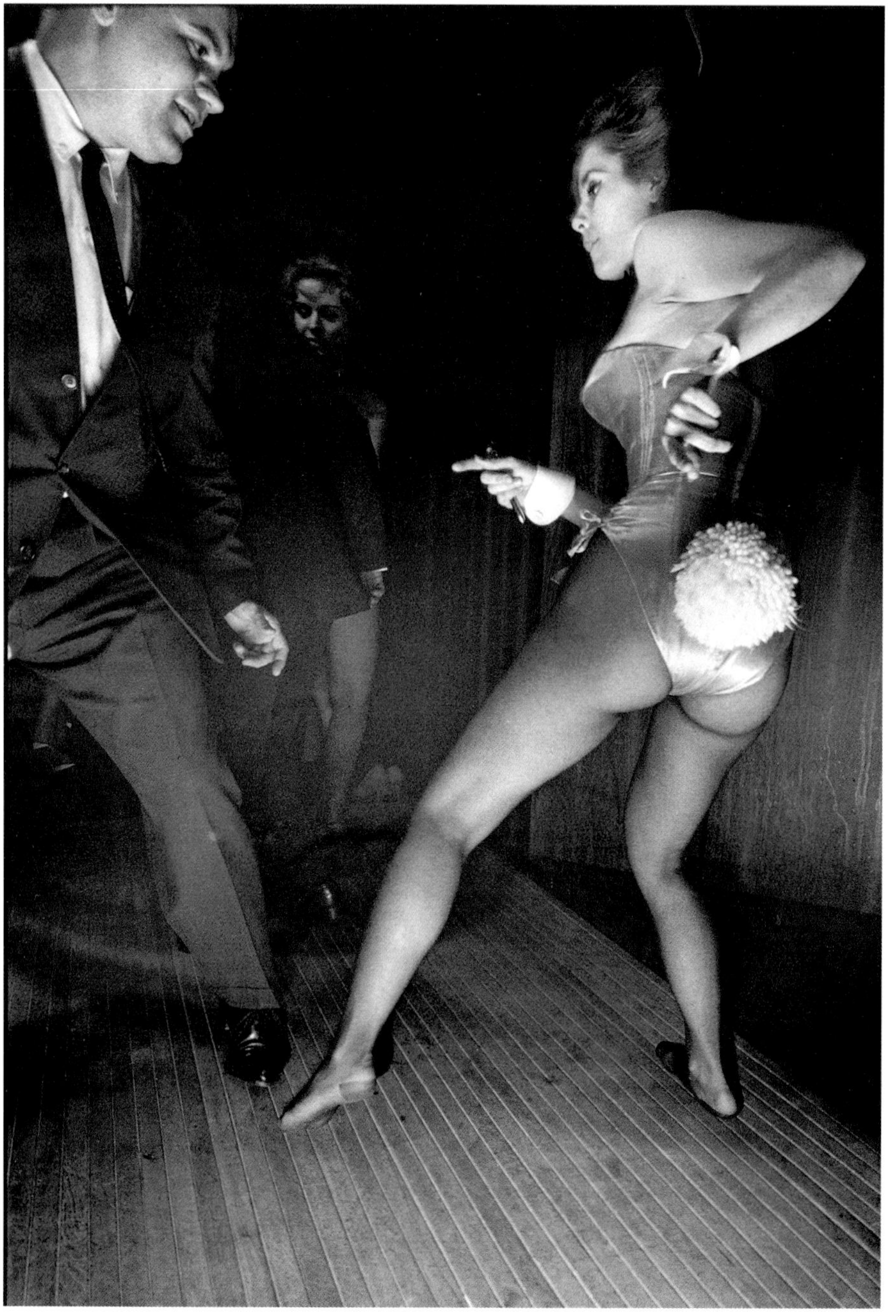

 Elliott Erwitt, USA, *États-Unis,* 1962.

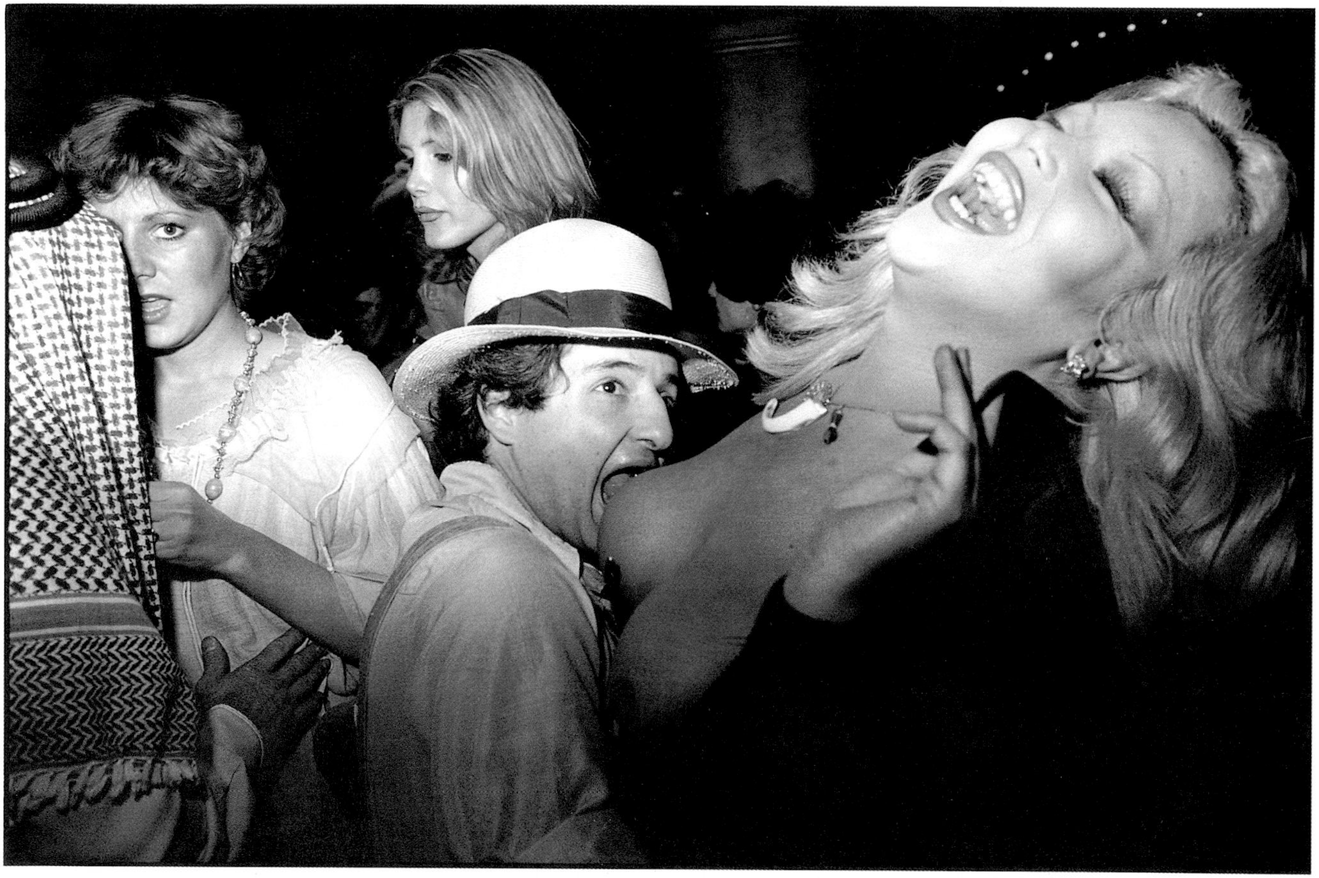

Guy Le Querrec, *France,* Frankreich, 1979.

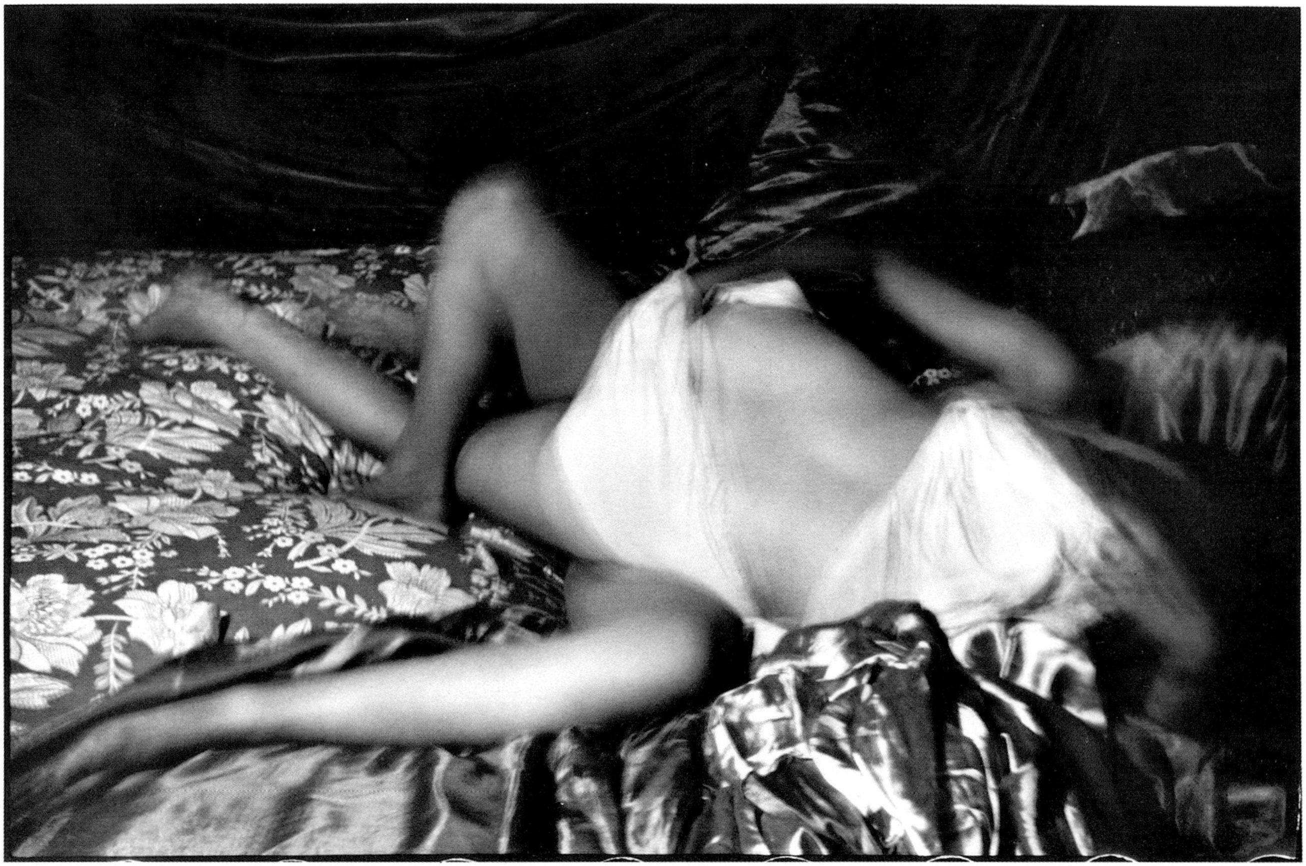

Henri Cartier-Bresson, Mexico, *Mexique,* Mexiko, 1934.

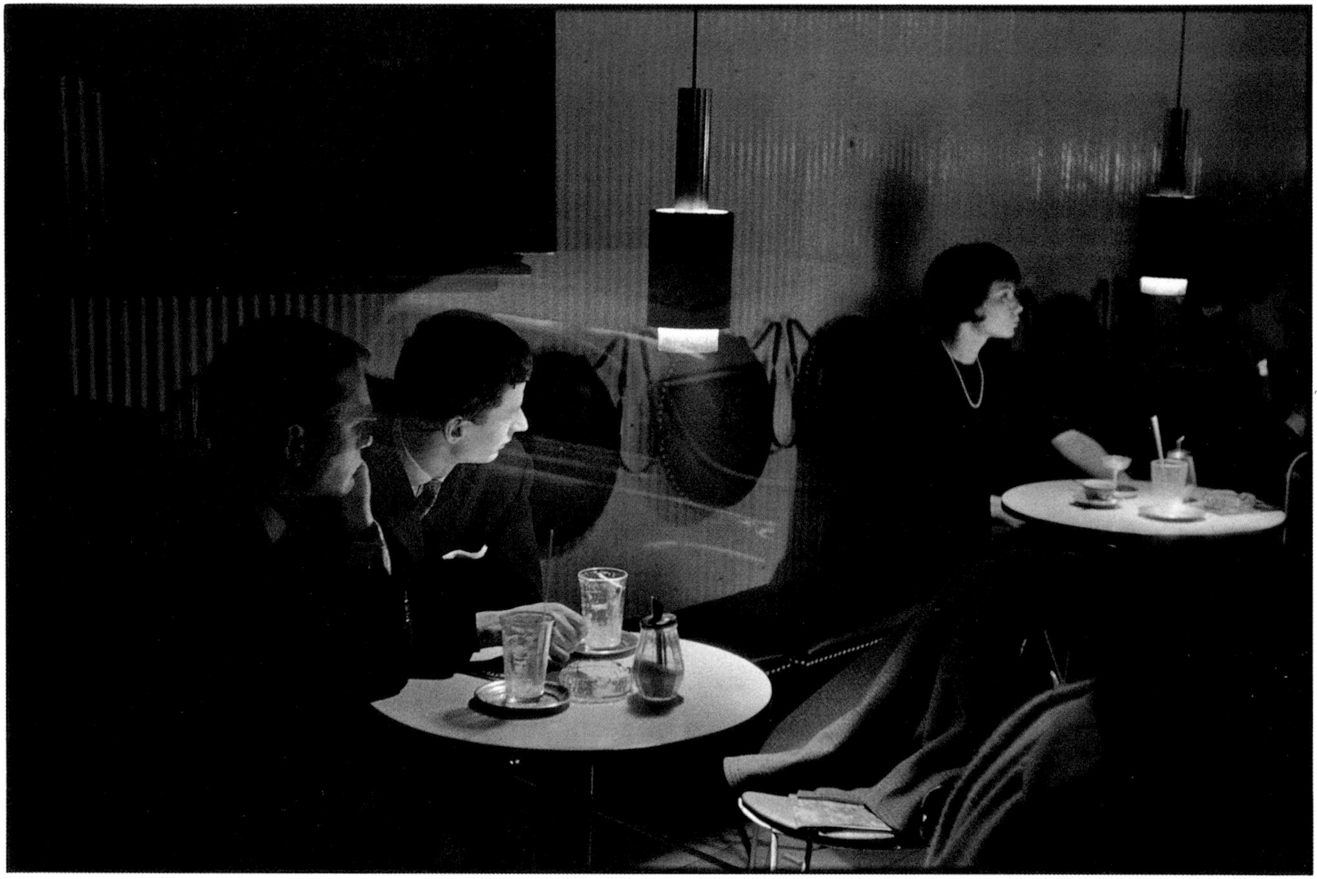

 René Burri, Federal Republic of Germany, *RFA,* Bundesrepublik Deutschland, 1961.

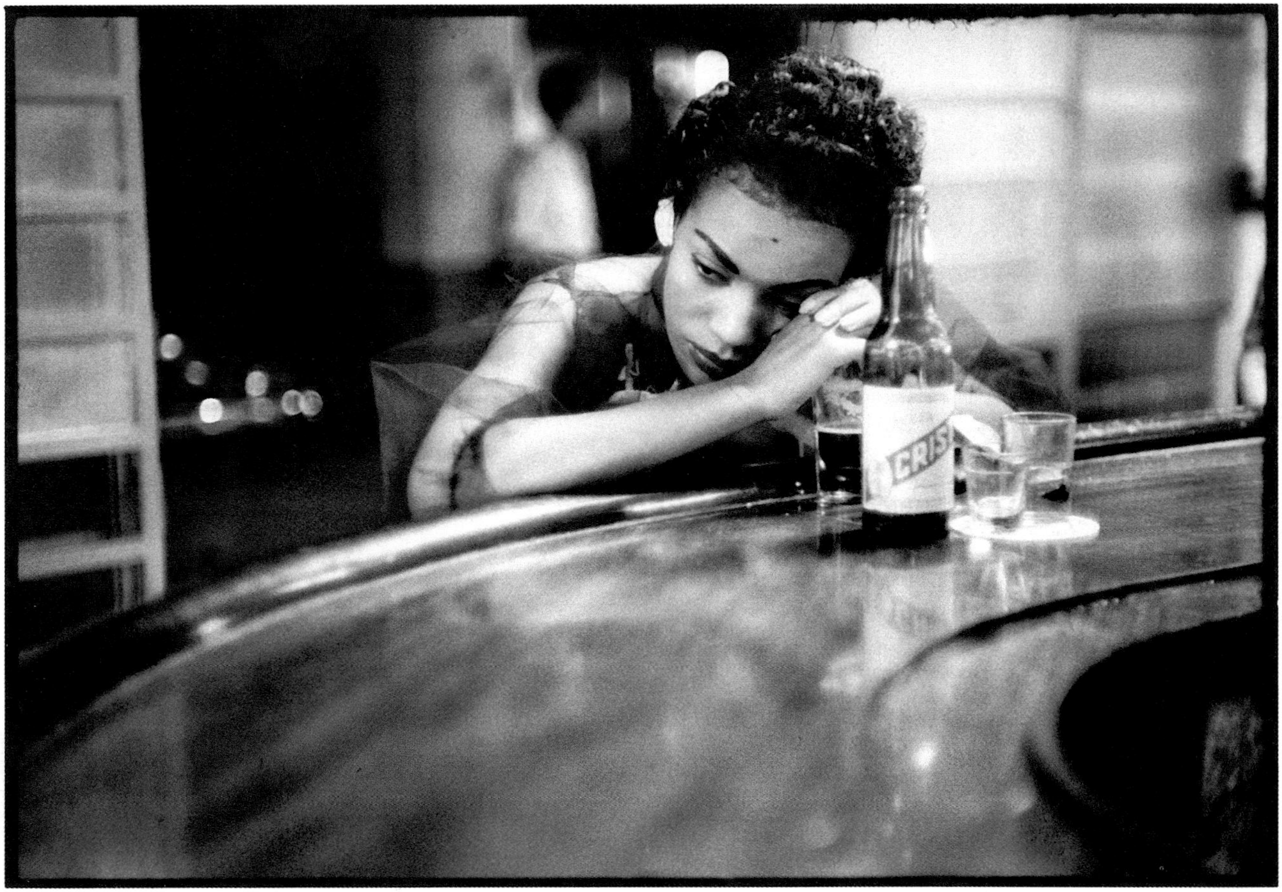

Eve Arnold, *Cuba,* Kuba, 1954.

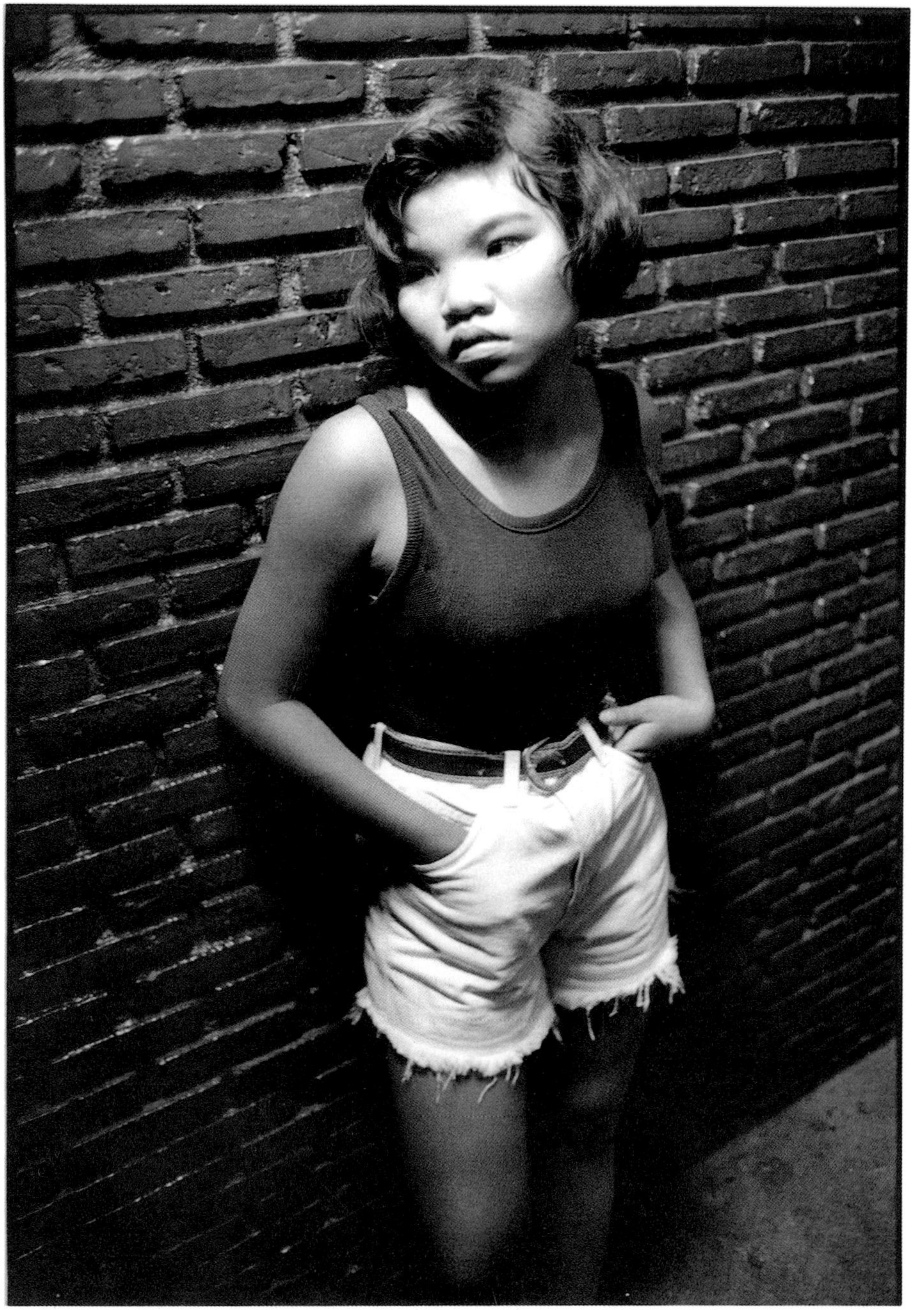

Patrick Zachmann, Thailand, *Thaïlande,* 1991.

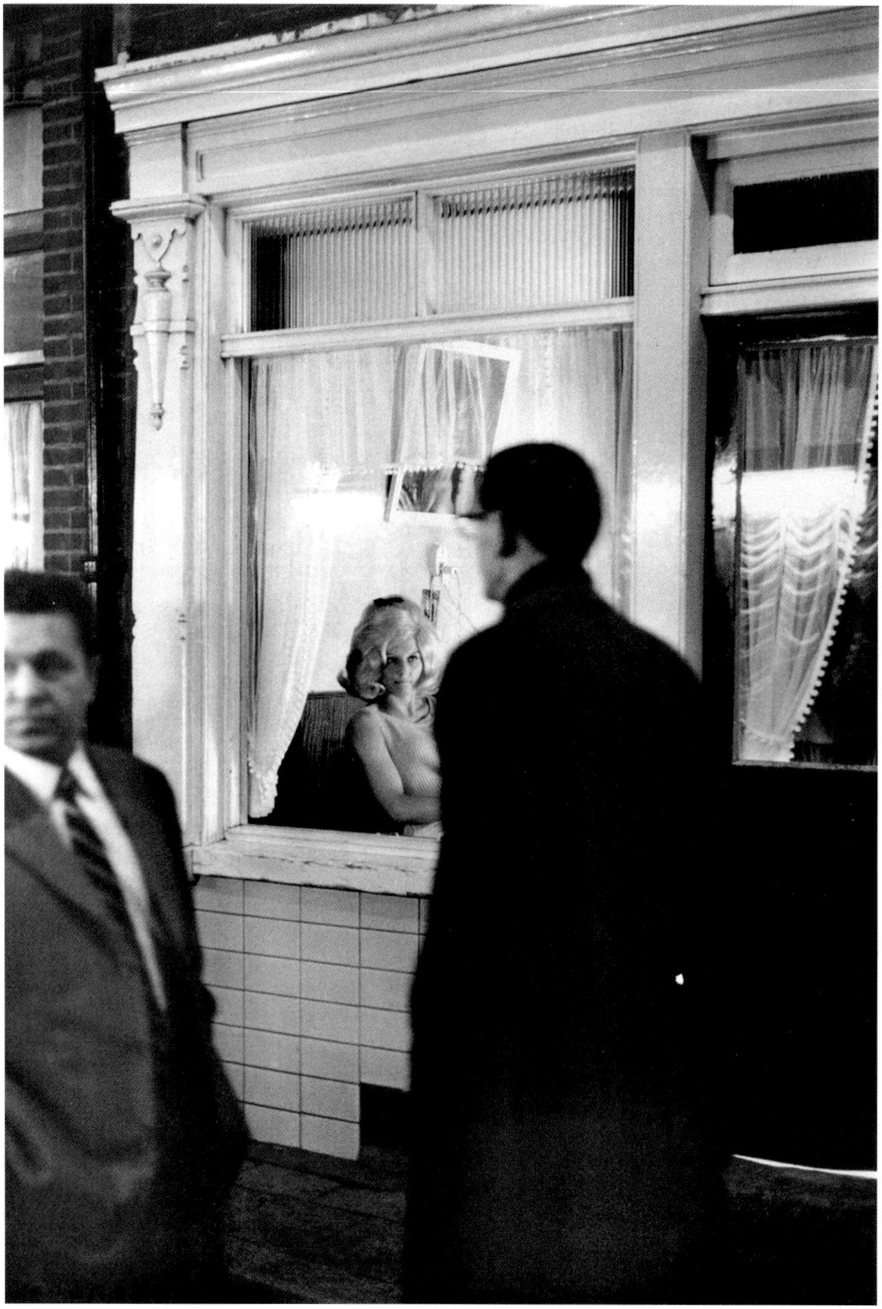

44 | Elliott Erwitt, The Netherlands, *Pays-Bas,* Niederlande, 1968.

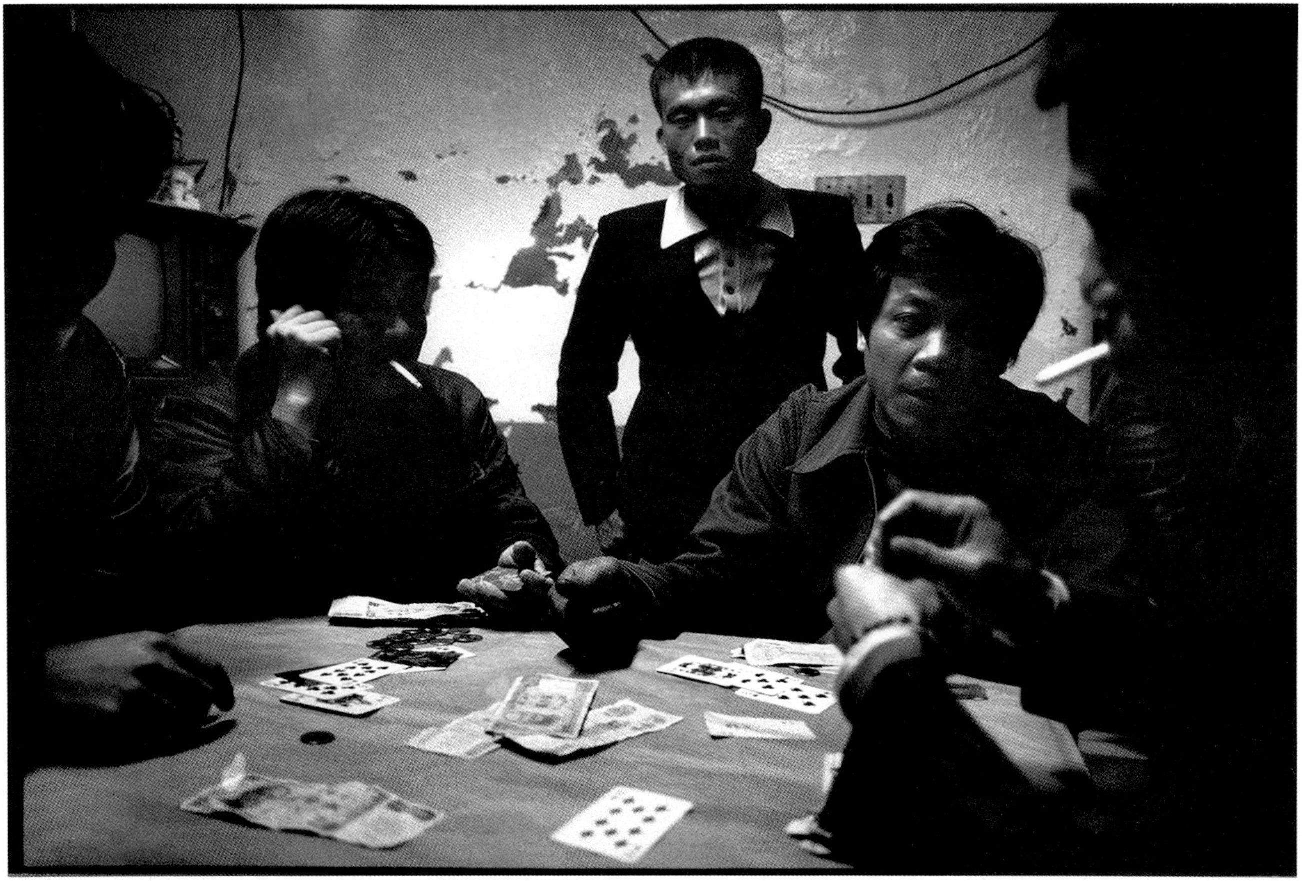

Patrick Zachmann, Taiwan, *Taïwan,* 1987.

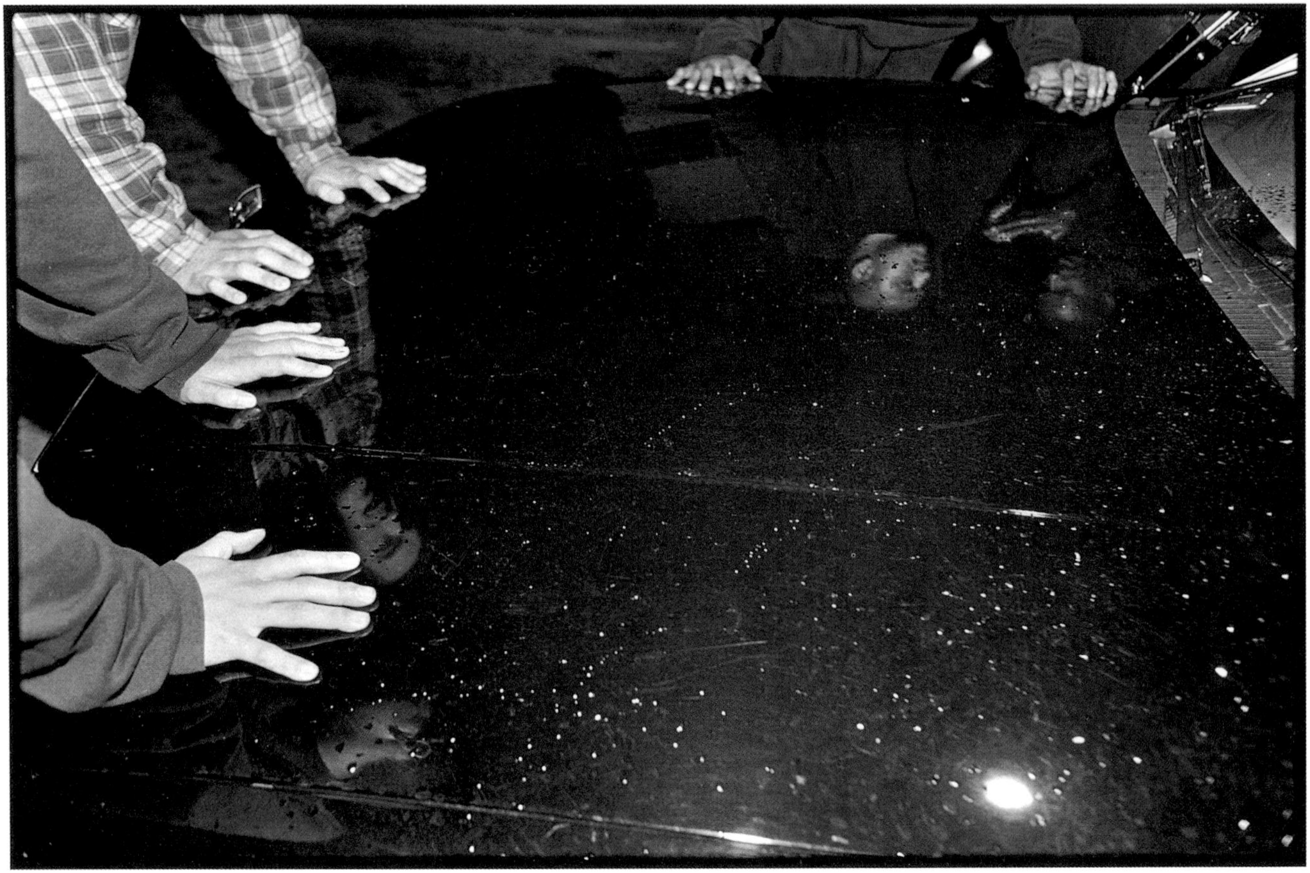

46 | James Nachtwey, USA, *États-Unis,* 1995.

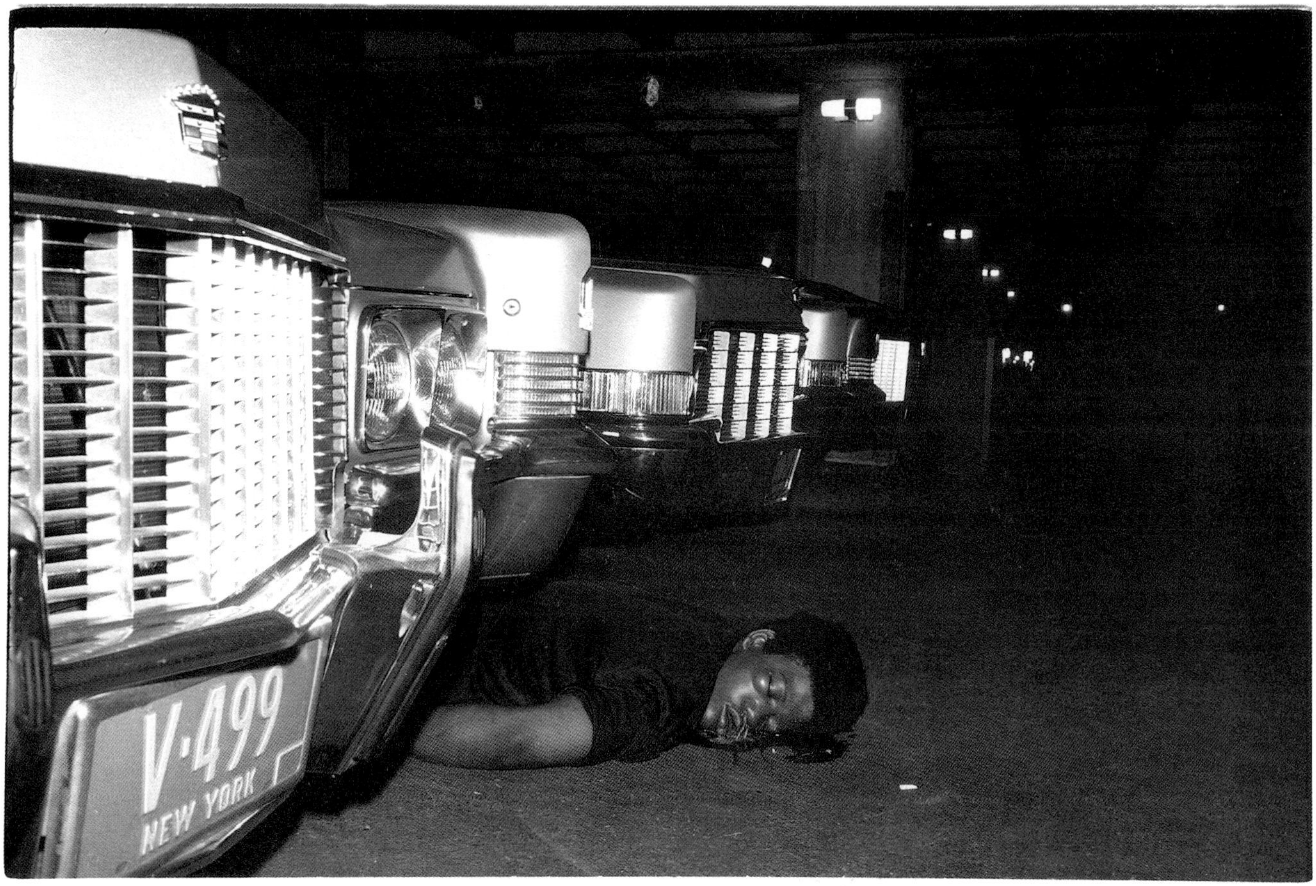

Leonard Freed, USA, *États-Unis,* 1972.

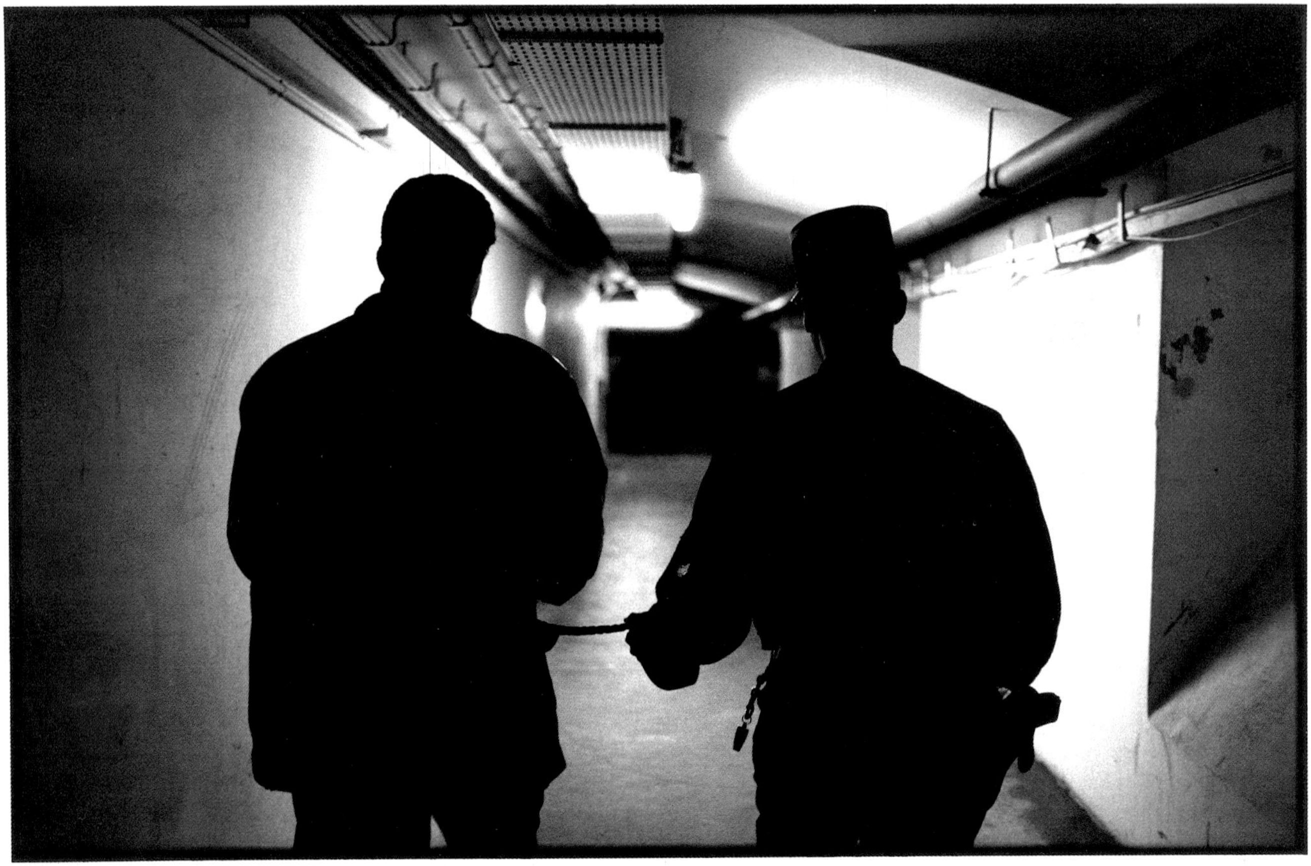

 Raymond Depardon, *France,* Frankreich, 1994.

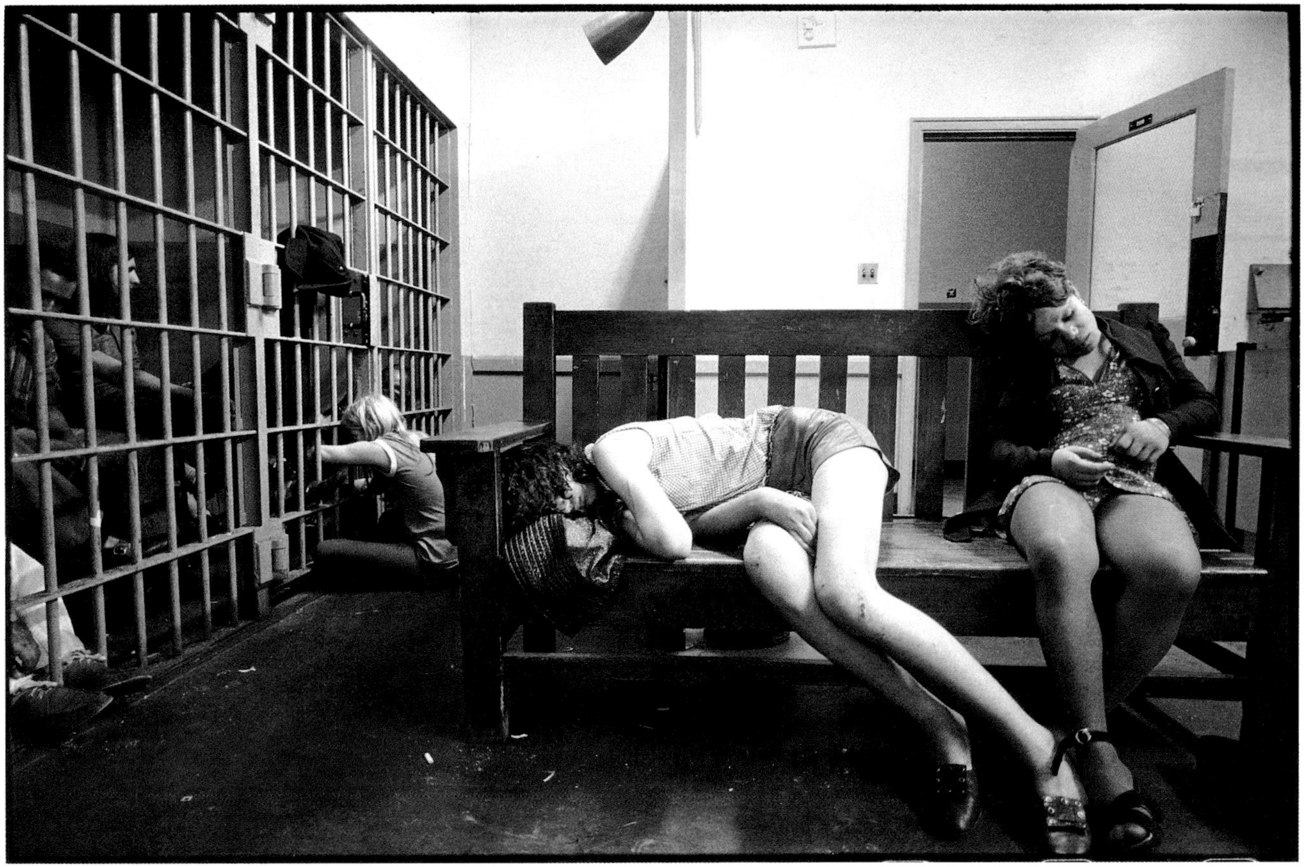

Leonard Freed, USA, *États-Unis,* 1972.

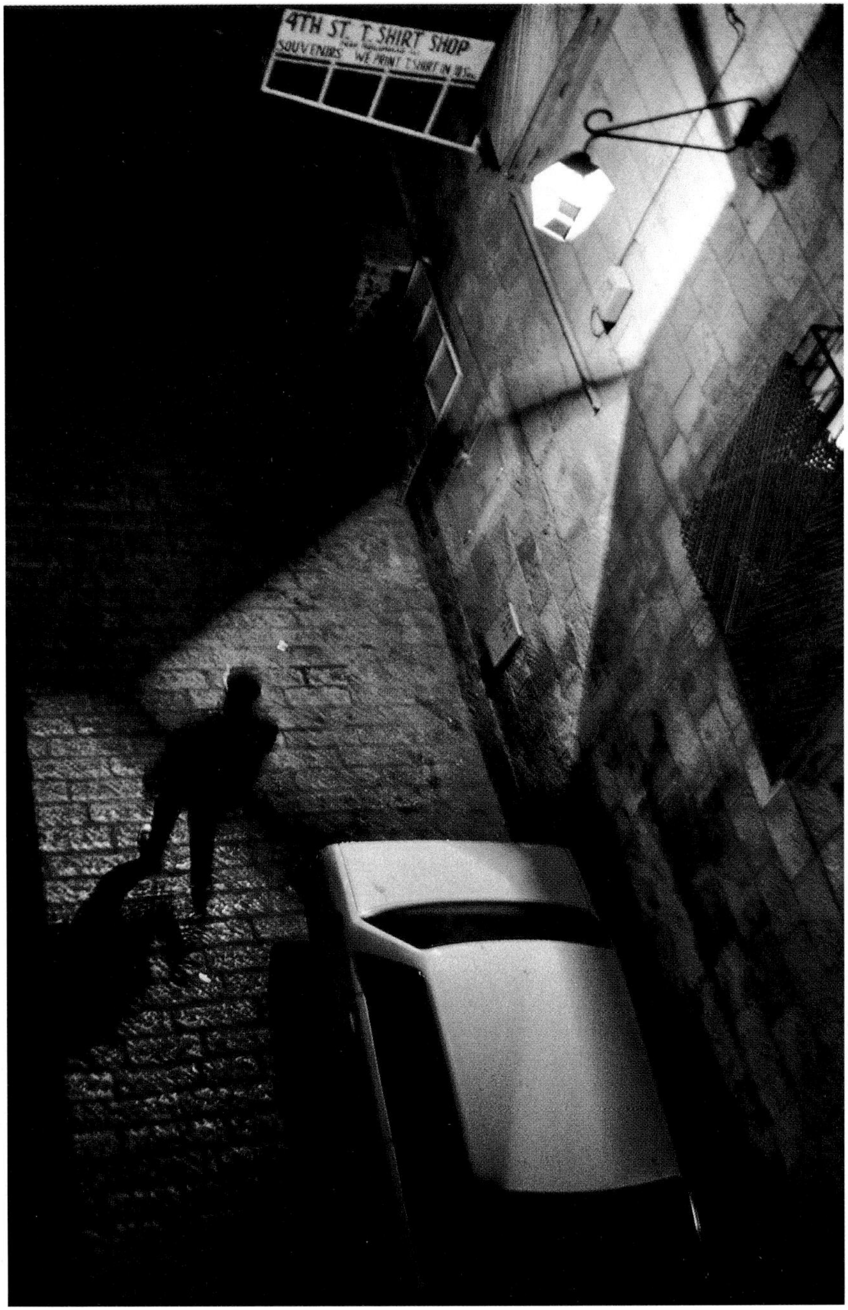

Larry Towell, Israel, *Israël,* 1993.

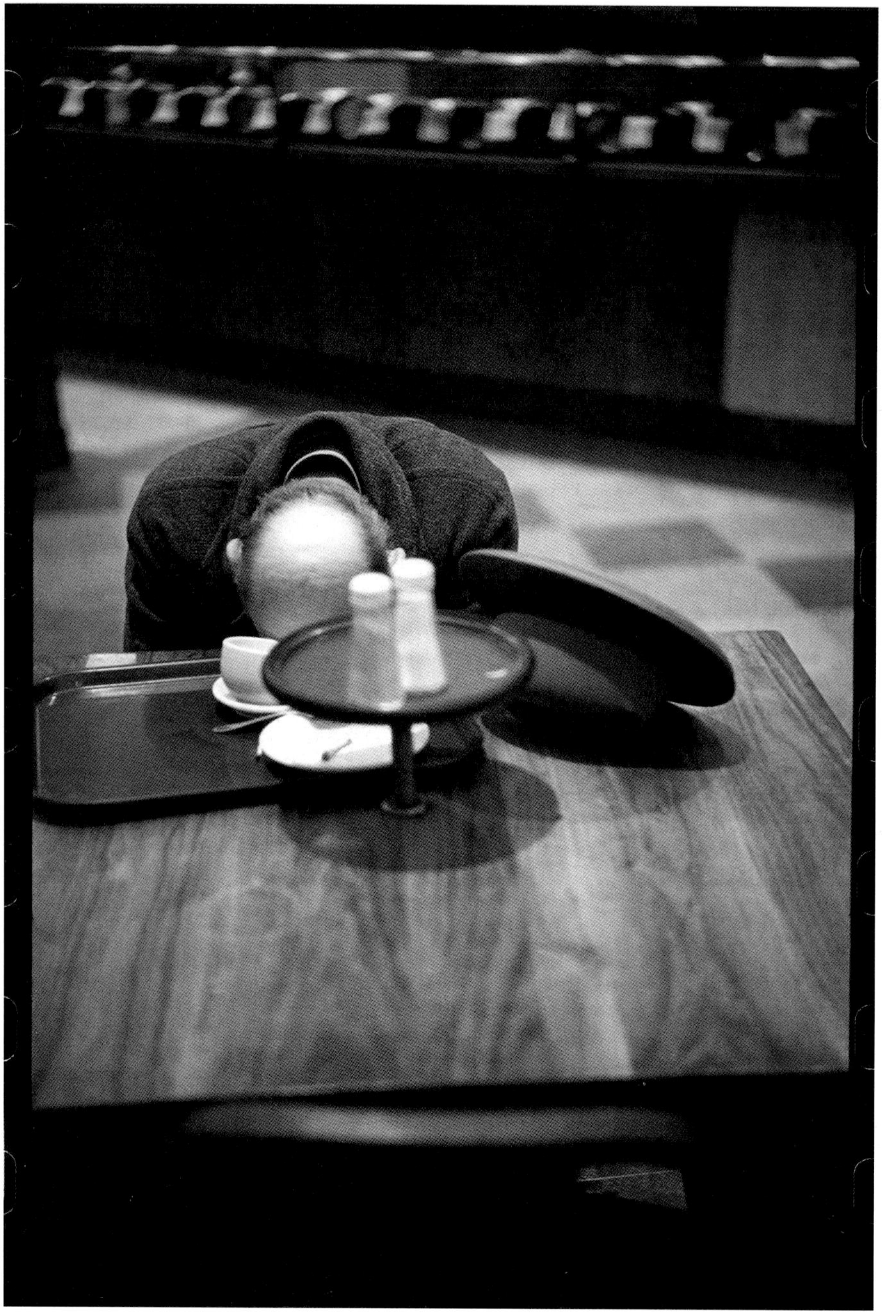

 Henri Cartier-Bresson, USA, *États-Unis,* 1946.

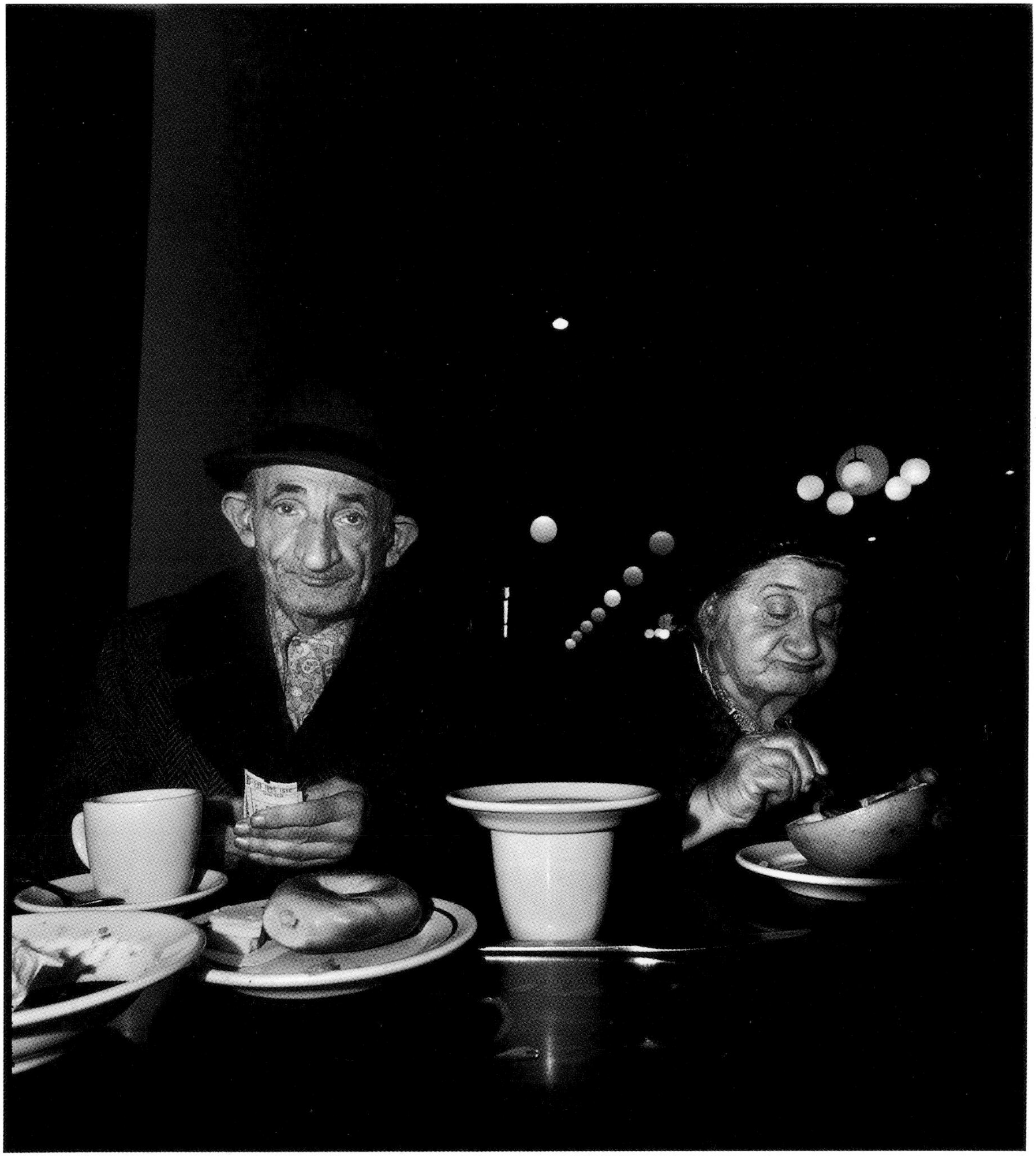

Bruce Davidson, USA, *États-Unis,* 1973.

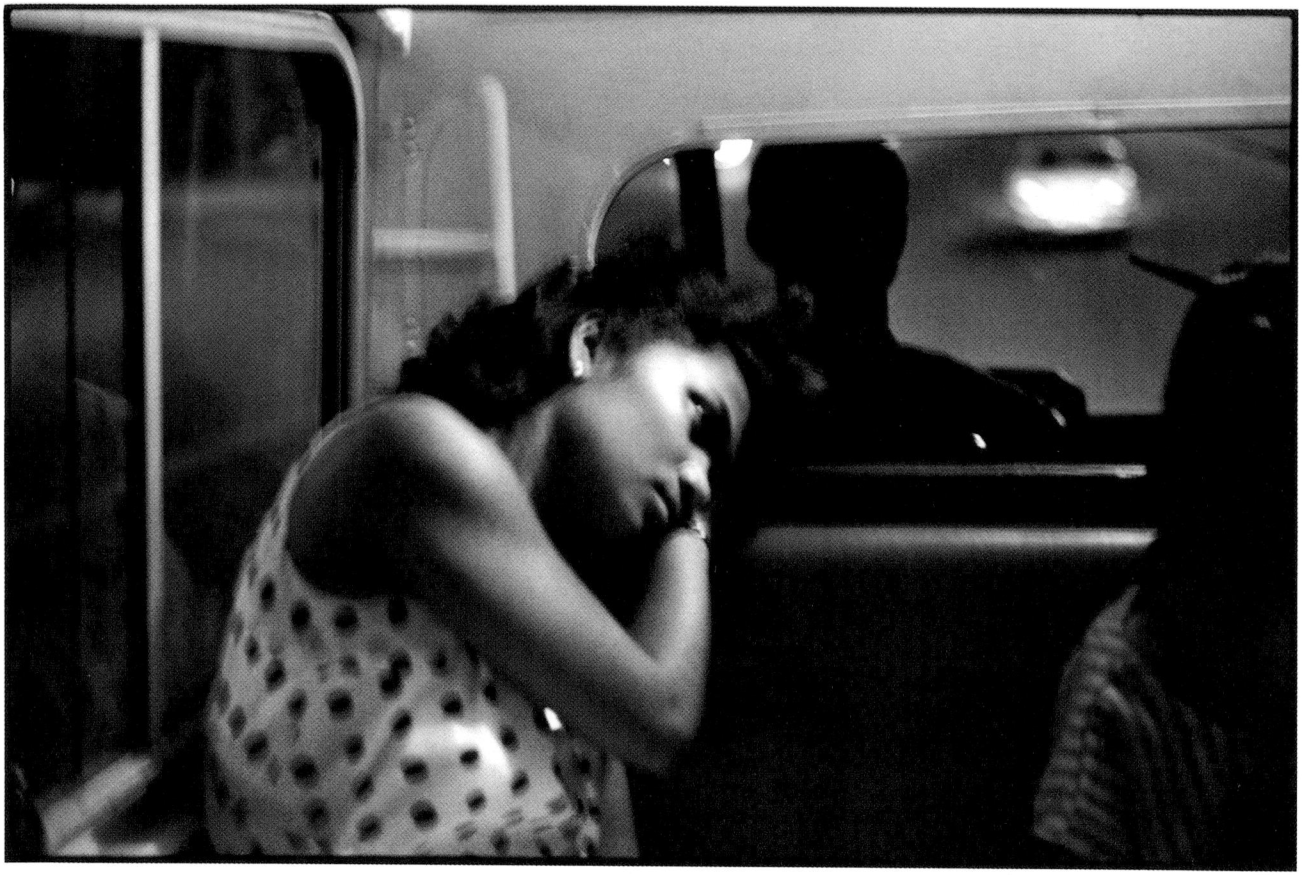

 Guy Le Querrec, Ivory Coast, *Côte-d'Ivoire,* Elfenbeinküste, 1986.

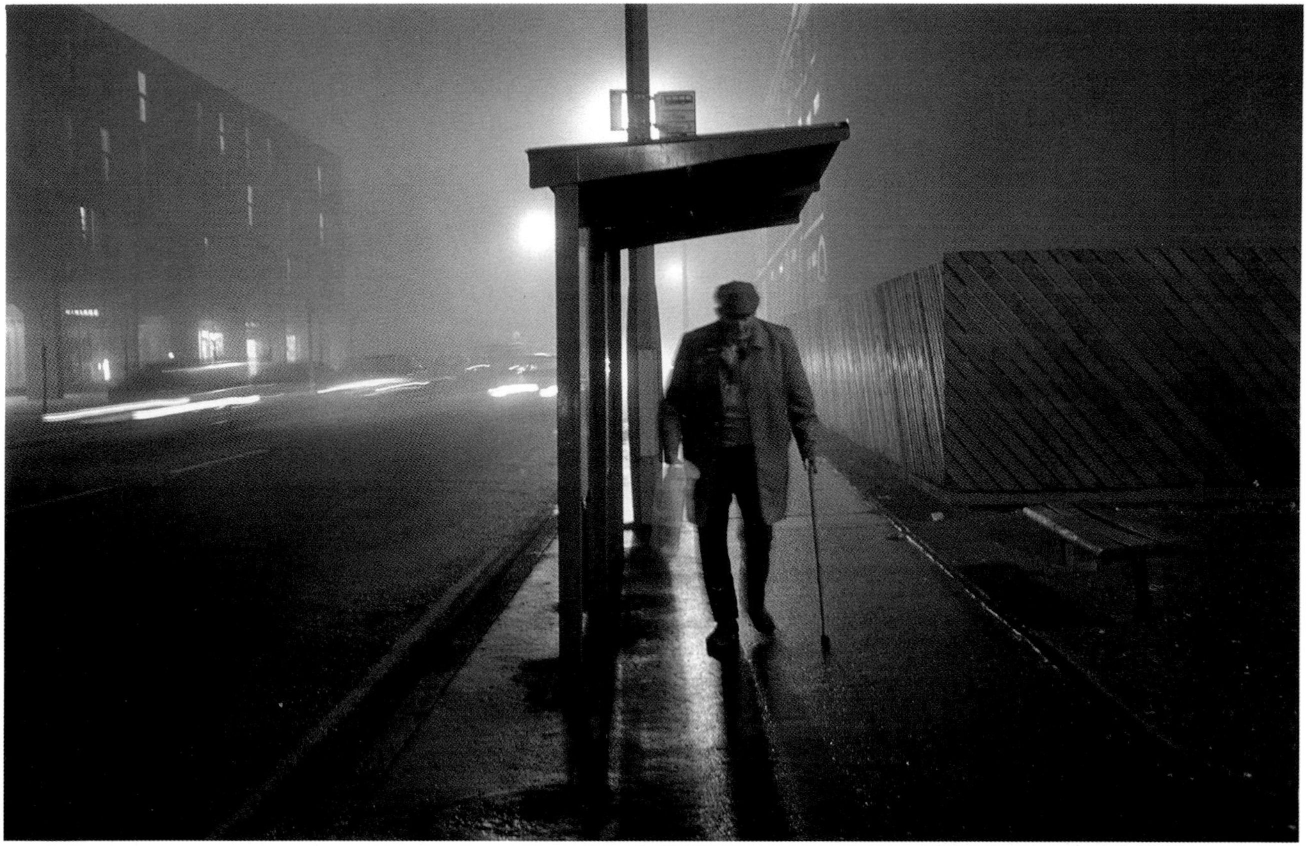

Peter Marlow, England, *Angleterre,* 1985.

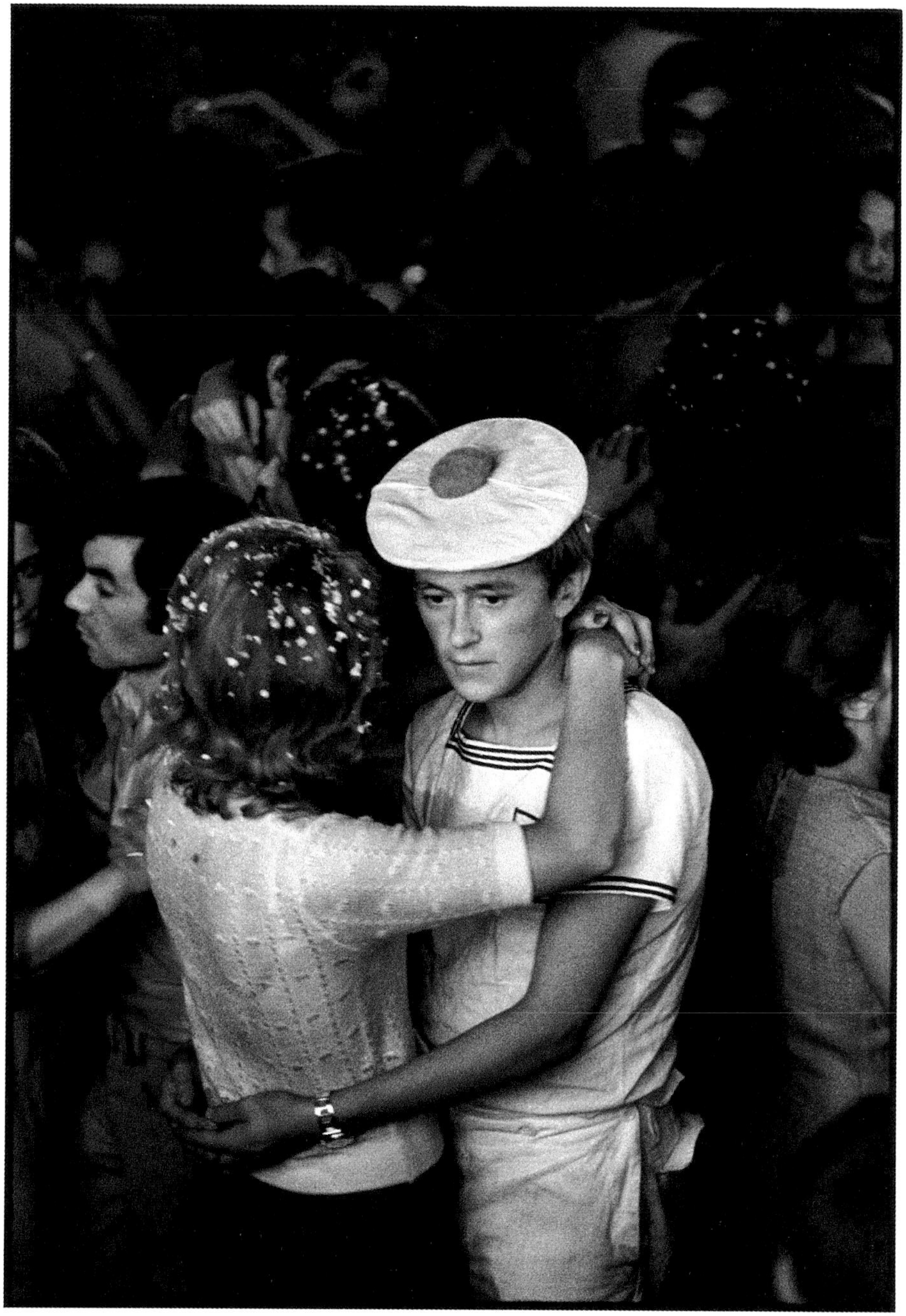

 Guy Le Querrec, *France,* Frankreich, 1971.

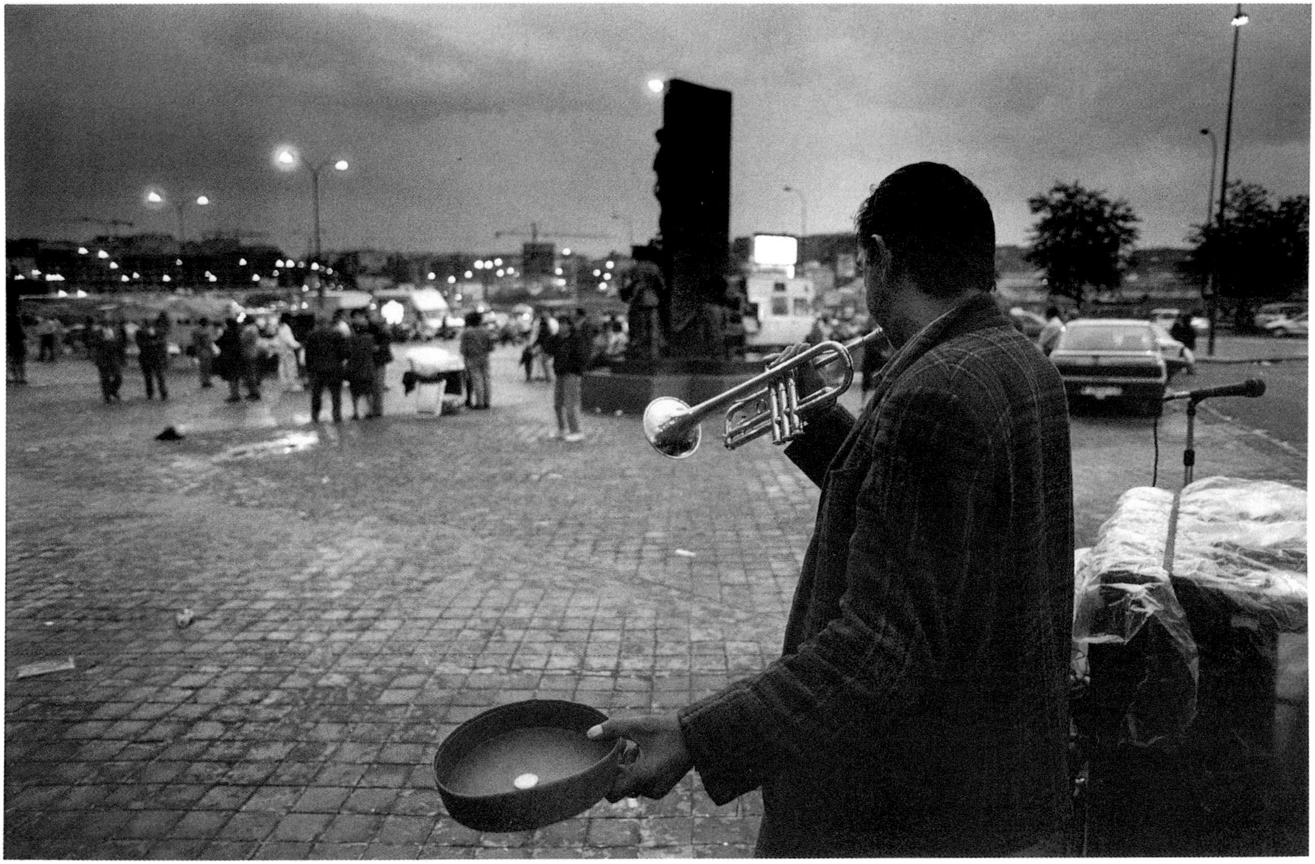

Ferdinando Scianna, Spain, *Espagne,* Spanien, 1993.

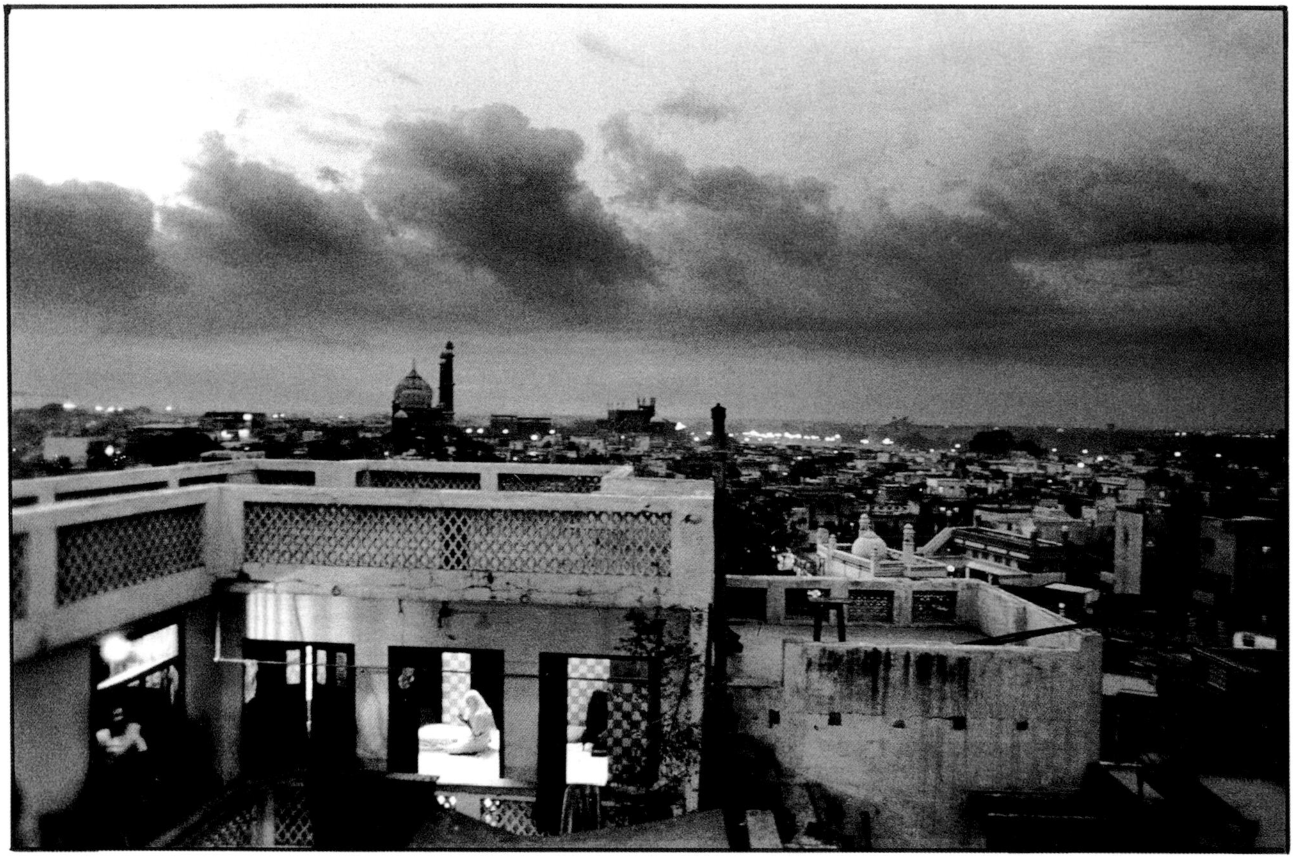

 Ferdinando Scianna, *France,* Frankreich, 1983.

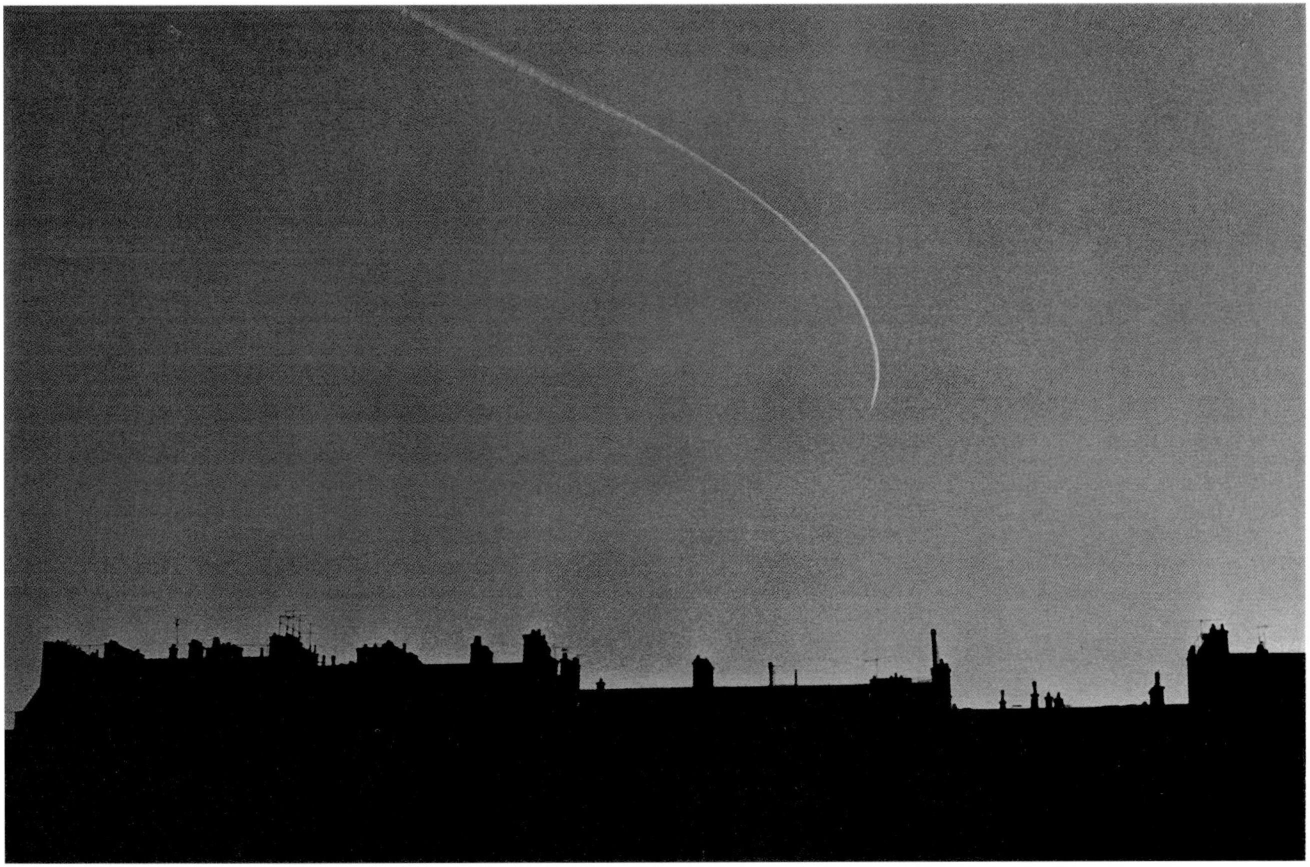

Raghu Rai, India, *Inde,* Indien, 1982.

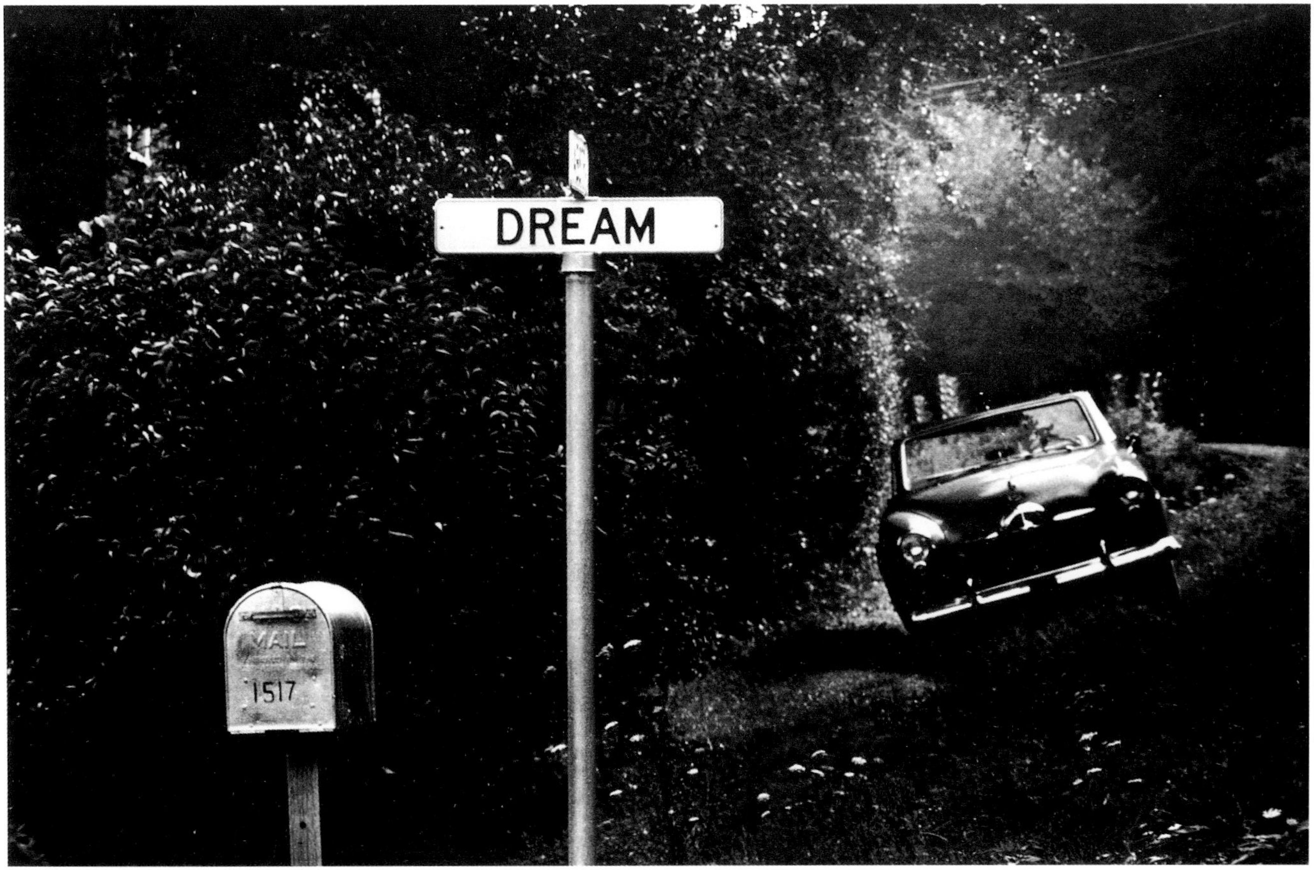

W. Eugene Smith, USA, *États-Unis,* 1955.

Page 5: Charleston, South Carolina, USA.
Hiroshi Hamaya, 1964.
Page 5 : *Charleston, Caroline du Sud, États-Unis.*
Hiroshi Hamaya, 1964.
Seite 5: Charleston, South Carolina, USA.
Hiroshi Hamaya, 1964.

Page 6-7: Fishing with cormorants, Guilin, China.
Hiroji Kubota, 1985.
Page 6-7 : *Pêche au cormoran, Guilin, Chine.*
Hiroji Kubota, 1985.
Seite 6-7: Kormoran Fishfang, Guilin, China.
Hiroji Kubota, 1985.

Page 8: St Mary's church on the island of South Ronaldsay, Scotland.
Peter Marlow, 1994.
Page 8 : *L'église de Sainte-Marie sur l'île de South Ronaldsay, Écosse.*
Peter Marlow, 1994.
Seite 8: Die Kirche Saint Mary auf der Insel South Ronaldsay, Schottland.
Peter Marlow, 1994.

Page 9: La Paz, Bolivia.
Chris Steele-Perkins, 1984.
Page 9 : *La Paz, Bolivie.*
Chris Steele-Perkins, 1984.
Seite 9: La Paz, Bolivien.
Chris Steele-Perkins, 1984.

Page 10: Bombay, Maharashtra, India.
Carl De Keyzer, 1985.
Page 10 : *Bombay, Maharashtra, Inde.*
Carl De Keyzer, 1985.
Seite 10: Bombay, Maharashtra, Indien.
Carl De Keyzer, 1985.

Page 11: The port of Algiers, Algeria.
Raymond Depardon, 1986.
Page 11 : *Le port d'Alger, Algérie.*
Raymond Depardon, 1986.
Seite 11: Der Hafen von Algier, Algerien.
Raymond Depardon, 1986.

Page 12: Valparaiso, Chile.
Sergio Larrain, 1963.
Page 12 : *Valparaiso, Chili.*
Sergio Larrain, 1963.
Seite 12: Valparaiso, Chile.
Sergio Larrain, 1963.

Page 13: Poole, England.
Ian Berry, 1974.
Page 13 : *Poole, Angleterre.*
Ian Berry, 1974.
Seite 13: Poole, England.
Ian Berry, 1974.

Page 14: Zurich, Switzerland.
Josef Koudelka, 1978.
Page 14 : *Zurich, Suisse.*
Josef Koudelka, 1978.
Seite 14: Zürich, Schweiz.
Josef Koudelka, 1978.

Page 15: New York, USA.
Ferdinando Scianna, 1985.
Page 15 : *New York, États-Unis.*
Ferdinando Scianna, 1985.
Seite 15: New York, USA.
Ferdinando Scianna, 1985.

Page 17: On the motorway. France.
Patrick Zachmann, 1983.
Page 17 : *Sur l'autoroute. France.*
Patrick Zachmann, 1983.
Seite 17: Auf der Autobahn. Frankreich.
Patrick Zachmann, 1983.

Page 18: West Berlin, Federal Republic of Germany.
René Burri, 1960.
Page 18 : *Berlin-Ouest, RFA.*
René Burri, 1960.
Seite 18: Westberlin, Bundesrepublik Deutschland.
René Burri, 1960.

Page 19: Venice, Italy.
Luc Delahaye, 1992.
Page 19 : *Venise, Italie.*
Luc Delahaye, 1992.
Seite 19: Venedig, Italien.
Luc Delahaye, 1992.

Page 20: Times Square. New York, USA.
Ernst Haas, 1962.
Page 20 : *Times Square. New York, États-Unis.*
Ernst Haas, 1962.
Seite 20: Times Square. New York, USA.
Ernst Haas, 1962.

Page 21: Denver, Colorado, USA.
René Burri, 1992.
Page 21 : *Denver, Colorado, États-Unis.*
René Burri, 1992.
Seite 21: Denver, Colorado, USA.
René Burri, 1992.

Page 23: Chinese New Year at Wenhzou. Zhejiang, China.
Patrick Zachmann, 1991.
Page 23 : *Nouvel an chinois à Wenhzou. Zhejiang, Chine.*
Patrick Zachmann, 1991.
Seite 23: Chinesisches Neujahrsfest in Wenhzou. Zhejiang, China.
Patrick Zachmann, 1991.

Page 24: New York, USA.
Gilles Peress, 1975.
Page 24 : *New York, États-Unis.*
Gilles Peress, 1975.
Seite 24: New York, USA.
Gilles Peress, 1975.

Page 25: Algiers, Algeria.
Abbas, 1982.
Page 25 : *Alger, Algérie.*
Abbas, 1982.
Seite 25: Algier, Algerien.
Abbas, 1982.

Page 26: Santiago, Chile.
Sergio Larrain, 1957.
Page 26 : *Santiago, Chili.*
Sergio Larrain, 1957.
Seite 26: Santiago, Chile.
Sergio Larrain, 1957.

Page 27 : *Le Val Fourré, Mantes-la-Jolie, France.*
Patrick Zachmann, 1990.
Seite 27: Le Val Fourré, Mantes-la-Jolie, Frankreich.
Patrick Zachmann, 1990.

Page 28: Chinatown, New York, USA.

Patrick Zachmann, 1987.
Page 28 : *Chinatown, New York, États-Unis.*
Patrick Zachmann, 1987.
Seite 28: Chinatown, New York, USA.
Patrick Zachmann, 1987.

Page 29 : *Paris, France.*
René Burri, 1962.
Seite 29: Paris, Frankreich.
René Burri, 1962.

Page 31: The Garnier opera house, Paris, France.
Raymond Depardon, 1985.
Page 31 : *Palais Garnier, Paris, France.*
Raymond Depardon, 1985.
Seite 31: Die Oper Palais Garnier, Paris, Frankreich.
Raymond Depardon, 1985.

Page 32: 14 July ball, Place de la Bastille. Paris, France.
Henri Cartier-Bresson, 1952.
Page 32 : *Bal du 14 Juillet place de la Bastille. Paris, France.*
Henri Cartier-Bresson, 1952.
Seite 32: Ball des 14. Juli an der Place de la Bastille. Paris, Frankreich.
Henri Cartier-Bresson, 1952.

Page 33 : *Café de Flore, Saint-Germain-des-Prés. Paris, France.*
Dennis Stock, 1958.
Seite 33: Café de Flore, Saint-Germain-des-Prés. Paris, Frankreich.
Dennis Stock, 1958.

Page 34: Transvestites. New York, USA.
Leonard Freed, 1995.
Page 34 : *Travestis. New York, États-Unis.*
Leonard Freed, 1995.
Seite 34: Transvestiten. New York, USA.
Leonard Freed, 1995.

Page 35: Stripteaser at the Crazy Horse Saloon. Paris, France.
Burt Glinn, 1956.
Page 35 : *Stripteaseuse au Crazy Horse Saloon. Paris, France.*
Burt Glinn, 1956.
Seite 35: Stripteasetänzerin des Crazy Horse Saloon. Paris, Frankreich.
Burt Glinn, 1956.

Page 36: Chicago, Illinois, USA.
Elliott Erwitt, 1962.
Page 36 : *Chicago, Illinois, États-Unis.*
Elliott Erwitt, 1962.
Seite 36: Chicago, Illinois, USA.
Elliott Erwitt, 1962.

Page 37: Mid-Lent carnival on the theme of the seven deadly sins. Le Palace, Paris, France.
Guy Le Querrec, 1979.
Page 37 : *Mi-carême sur le thème des sept péchés capitaux. Le Palace, Paris, France.*
Guy Le Querrec, 1979.
Seite 37: Mittfastenzeit-Karneval; Thema: Die sieben Todsünden. Le Palace, Paris, Frankreich.
Guy Le Querrec, 1979.

Page 39: Mexico.
Henri Cartier-Bresson, 1934.
Page 39 : *Mexique.*
Henri Cartier-Bresson, 1934.
Seite 39: Mexiko.
Henri Cartier-Bresson, 1934.

Page 40: Cologne, Federal Republic of Germany.
René Burri, 1961.
Page 40 : *Cologne, RFA.*
René Burri, 1961.
Seite 40: Köln, Bundesrepublik Deutschland.
René Burri, 1961.

Page 41: "Hostess" in a brothel. Havana, Cuba.
Eve Arnold, 1954.
Page 41 : *Entraîneuse dans un bordel. La Havane, Cuba.*
Eve Arnold, 1954.
Seite 41: Animiermädchen in einem Bordell. Havanna, Kuba.
Eve Arnold, 1954.

Page 43: Soy Nana district, Bangkok, Thailand.
Patrick Zachmann, 1991.
Page 43 : *Quartier Soy Nana, Bangkok, Thaïlande.*
Patrick Zachmann, 1991.
Seite 43: Stadtviertel Soy Nana, Bangkok, Thailand.
Patrick Zachmann, 1991.

Page 44: Amsterdam, The Netherlands.
Elliott Erwitt, 1968.
Page 44 : *Amsterdam, Pays-Bas.*
Elliott Erwitt, 1968.
Seite 44: Amsterdam, Niederlande.
Elliott Erwitt, 1968.

Page 45: Gamblers in Taishung. Taiwan.
Patrick Zachmann, 1987.
Page 45 : *Joueurs à Taishung. Taïwan.*
Patrick Zachmann, 1987.
Seite 45: Spieler in Taishung. Taiwan.
Patrick Zachmann, 1987.

Page 46: Suspects frisked by the police on the bonnet of a car reported stolen. Los Angeles, California, USA.
James Nachtwey, 1995.
Page 46 : *Suspects fouillés par la police sur le capot d'une voiture signalée comme volée. Los Angeles, Californie, États-Unis.*
James Nachtwey, 1995.
Seite 46: Von der Polizei auf der Motorhaube eines als gestohlen signalisierten Autos durchsuchte Verdächtige. Los Angeles, Kalifornien, USA.
James Nachtwey, 1995.

Page 47: Gang warfare in a Harlem garage. New York, USA.
Leonard Freed, 1972.
Page 47 : *Guerre de gangs dans un garage de Harlem. New York, États-Unis.*
Leonard Freed, 1972.
Seite 47: Krieg der Gangs in einer Harlemer Garage. New York, USA.
Leonard Freed, 1972.

Page 48: Underground

detentioncentre at police headquarters, used for holding people on remand.
Paris, France.
Raymond Depardon, 1994.
Page 48 : *Centre de détention souterrain de la préfecture de police utilisé pour les personnes en détention provisoire.*
Paris, France.
Raymond Depardon, 1994.
Seite 48: Unterirdisches Zentrum für einstweilige Verwahrung der Polizeipräfektur.
Paris, Frankreich.
Raymond Depardon, 1994.

■ **Page 49:** Teenage girls arrested by the police. New York, USA.
Leonard Freed, 1972.
Page 49 : *Adolescentes arrêtées par la police.*
New York, États-Unis.
Leonard Freed, 1972.
Seite 49: Von der Polizei festgenommene Jugendliche.
New York, USA.
Leonard Freed, 1972.

■ **Page 51:** The Arab quarter, East Jerusalem, Israel.
Larry Towell, 1993.
Page 51 : *Quartiers arabes, Jérusalem-Est, Israël.*
Larry Towell, 1993.
Seite 51: Arabische Viertel, Ostjerusalem, Israel.
Larry Towell, 1993.

■ **Page 52:** Café on 2nd Avenue, Brooklyn, New York, USA.
Henri Cartier-Bresson, 1946.
Page 52 : *Café sur la 2ᵉ Avenue, Brooklyn, New York, États-Unis.*
Henri Cartier-Bresson, 1946.
Seite 52: Café an der 2nd Avenue, Brooklyn, New York, USA.
Henri Cartier-Bresson, 1946.

■ **Page 53:** Cafeteria, New York, USA.
Bruce Davidson, 1973.
Page 53 : *Cafétéria, New York, États-Unis.*
Bruce Davidson, 1973.
Seite 53: Cafeteria, New York, USA.
Bruce Davidson, 1973.

■ **Page 54:** "Découvertes 86" festival, annual song contest organised by Radio France International (RFI), the listeners' prize; the winner Rajaofara Malalatiana, called Lalatiana, a Madagascan singer, in the mini bus between Yamoussoukro and Abidjan after a television broadcast. Ivory Coast.
Guy Le Querrec, 1986.
Page 54 : *Festival « Découvertes 86 », concours annuel de la chanson organisé par Radio France international (RFI), prix des auditeurs ; la lauréate Rajaofara Malalatiana, dite Lalatiana, chanteuse malgache, dans le mini-bus entre Yamoussoukro et Abidjan après une émission de télévision. Côte-d'Ivoire.*
Guy Le Querrec, 1986.
Seite 54: Festival „Découvertes 86", jährlicher, von Radio France International (RFI) organisierter Chanson-Wettbewerb mit dem Hörerpreisverleih; die Gewinnerin Rajaofara Malalatiana, Lalatiania genannt, eine Malgache-Sängerin, in einem Kleinbus zwischen Yamoussoukro und Abidjan nach einer Fernsehsendung. Elfenbeinküste.
Guy Le Querrec, 1986.

■ **Page 55:** Liverpool, England.
Peter Marlow, 1985.
Page 55 : *Liverpool, Angleterre.*
Peter Marlow, 1985.
Seite 56: Liverpool, England.
Peter Marlow, 1985.

■ **Page 56:** The "Sparkling Night" ball in front of the open-air theatre. Nice, France.
Guy Le Querrec, 1971.
Page 56 : *Bal de « la nuit scintillante » devant le théâtre de verdure. Nice, France.*
Guy Le Querrec, 1971.
Seite 56: Der Ball „Funkelnde Nacht" vor dem Open-air-Theater.
Nizza, Frankreich. Guy Le Querrec, 1971.

■ **Page 57:** Madrid, Spain.
Ferdinando Scianna, 1993.
Page 57 : *Madrid, Espagne.*
Ferdinando Scianna, 1993.
Seite 57: Madrid, Spanien.
Ferdinando Scianna, 1993.

■ **Page 58 :** *Paris, France.*
Ferdinando Scianna, 1983.
Seite 58: Paris, Frankreich.
Ferdinando Scianna, 1983.

■ **Page 59:** Evening prayer.
Delhi, India.
Raghu Rai, 1982.
Page 59 : *Prière du soir.*
Delhi, Inde.
Raghu Rai, 1982.
Seite 59: Abendgebet.
Delhi, Indien.
Raghu Rai, 1982.

■ **Page 61:** Pittsburgh, Pennsylvania, USA.
W. Eugene Smith, 1955.
Page 61 : *Pittsburgh, Pennsylvanie, États-Unis.*
W. Eugene Smith, 1955.
Seite 61: Pittsburgh, Pennsylvania, USA.
W. Eugene Smith, 1955.